Praise for *The Complete Game*

"Darling comes up a winner in his rookie writing effort. There's plenty to satisfy Met fans—and more. . . . In his typically engaging style, [Darling] lets the reader in on the parts of the game fans can't see from the stands or on their TVs."

—*New York Post*

"A pitcher's answer to Ted Williams's classic, *The Science of Hitting* . . . Thoughtful and lively . . . [Darling is] an affable, frank, and witty guide."

—Bruce Handy, *The New York Times Book Review*

"Darling offers pitches and outcomes . . . from ten selected games in his career. . . . Among them are enough oddities and thrilling turns of baseball to make a reader glad to be here and—well, not out there."

—*The New Yorker*

"Darling's little gem of a book immediately takes its place alongside *Ball Four* and *Moneyball* as a classic, and the best account ever of the way pitchers think."

—Joseph J. Ellis, author of *American Creation*

"Totally absorbing. Ron Darling takes us inside the mind of a pitcher, and a funny, thoughtful, and observant one at that."

—Kevin Baker, author of *Sometimes You See It Coming* and *Paradise Alley*

"This is a book for all of Baseball Nation to cherish. . . . Darling moves adeptly between his own experience on the mound and his probing analysis of the art and psychology of pitching to offer us a rare glimpse inside the world of the loneliest man on the field. The result is the pitching equivalent of Ted Williams's *The Science of Hitting*."

—Jonathan Mahler, author of *Ladies and Gentlemen, the Bronx Is Burning*

GAME 7, 1986

RON DARLING

WITH DANIEL PAISNER

GAME 7, 1986

FAILURE AND TRIUMPH IN THE BIGGEST GAME OF MY LIFE

 St. Martin's Griffin ⚞ New York

GAME 7, 1986. Copyright © 2016 by Ron Darling. All rights reserved. Printed in the United States of America. For information, address St. Martin's Press, 175 Fifth Avenue, New York, N.Y. 10010.

www.stmartins.com

Photo on pp. iv–v © Getty Images

Designed by Omar Chapa

The Library of Congress has cataloged the hardcover edition as follows:

Names: Darling, Ron, author. | Paisner, Daniel.
Title: Game 7, 1986 : failure and triumph in the biggest game of my life / Ron Darling with Daniel Paisner.
Description: New York : St. Martin's Press, 2016. | Includes index.
Identifiers: LCCN 2016001118| ISBN 9781250069191 (hardcover) |
    ISBN 9781250106971 (signed edition) | ISBN 9781466878105 (e-book)
Subjects: LCSH: Darling, Ron. | Baseball players—United States—Biography. |
    Pitchers (Baseball)—United States—Biography. | New York Mets (Baseball team)—
    History. | BISAC: SPORTS & RECREATION / Baseball / Essays & Writings. |
    BIOGRAPHY & AUTOBIOGRAPHY / Sports.
Classification: LCC GV865.D37 A3 2016 | DDC 796.357092—dc23
LC record available at http://lccn.loc.gov/2016001118

ISBN 978-1-250-11874-5 (trade paperback)

Our books may be purchased in bulk for promotional, educational, or business use. Please contact your local bookseller or the Macmillan Corporate and Premium Sales Department at 1-800-221-7945, extension 5442, or by e-mail at MacmillanSpecialMarkets@macmillan .com.

First St. Martin's Griffin Edition: April 2017

10 9 8 7 6 5 4 3 2 1

I've had a great life. This book is just a sneak peek into it. But none of it would have happened without my parents— Ron Sr. and Mikina.

CONTENTS

ACKNOWLEDGMENTS

One of the things I miss from my playing days is the team aspect of the game. There was this powerful, enveloping feeling—up and down the bench, in and out of the clubhouse, on and off the road—that we were all in this thing together. And we were—oh, definitely, we were. Happily, I can find the same esprit de corps in the broadcast booth at SNY, at TBS, and at the MLB Network—and here it is again, on full display, as I dip my toe in these publishing waters. I am grateful for the encouragement and guidance of Mel Berger at William Morris Endeavor and Michael Homler at St. Martin's Press, and for the time and talents of my friend and writing partner Dan Paisner. This book might have been pulled from the recesses of memory, but it was spit-shined and polished by a number of talented, dedicated individuals at St. Martin's—including Lauren Jablonski, Ken Silver, Joy Gannon, Joseph Rinaldi, Laura Clark, Jimmy Iacobelli, Alastair Hayes, Martin Quinn, Sally Richardson, George Witte, and Jason Prince . . . a huge shout-out to all. And finally, to my friends and family members and former teammates, thank you for enriching my life and helping me to recall some of these tucked-away stories from that glorious season so long ago.

There's three things you can do in a baseball game. You can win or you can lose or it can rain.

— CASEY STENGEL, HALL OF FAME MANAGER

A baseball game is simply a nervous breakdown divided into nine innings.

— EARL WILSON, FORMER MAJOR LEAGUE PITCHER

GAME 7, 1986

INTRODUCTION

BE CAREFUL WHAT YOU WISH FOR

Like a lot of former ballplayers' time in the sun, mine was marked by a moment, a game, a streak, a season. For me, those sun-drenched benchmarks found me as a member of the 1986 New York Mets, a championship team that stamped my time in the game, and yet I was never much interested in writing about that one wondrous season, mainly because I wasn't much interested in telling the wild stories people seemed to want to hear.

We made a lot of headlines that year, and in all the years since. Some of the noise we made had to do with baseball, but a lot of it was just noise. When you're young and stupid and on top of your game, you find ways of convincing yourself you'll always be young and stupid and on top of your game. You stick your chest out, you strut, because you've been conditioned to stick your chest out, to strut. You move without thinking, make a lot of decisions you'd like to take back, tell yourself the baseball part can be switched to autopilot while you and your teammates find a bunch of new ways to enjoy the ride.

And so the "bad boy" image that attached to that team wasn't something I cared to perpetuate. I'd lived it—I didn't need to revisit it. Whatever happened outside the lines that year was for me and my teammates—youthful misadventures to file away and maybe even forget—but what happened *inside* the lines was certainly something special, something to be cherished and considered.

So I did—privately.

Lately, as the thirtieth anniversary of the 1986 World Series approached, I began to look back on that time in my life through a wistful lens, and it occurred to me that I was uniquely positioned to shine a particular light on that summer, on those postseason games that have been etched into baseball lore . . . even on some of those bad boy–type shenanigans that, taken in context, helped to shape the personality of that championship team. I started to realize that what most people remember when they think of the 1986 Mets is Game 6 of the World Series, which has by now taken on the hue of a Bernard Malamud novel on steroids. What they remember, specifically, was just one play—and they remember it with brushstrokes keyed to their allegiance.

Recall, the Sox had been up by two runs going into the bottom of the tenth inning, leading the series three games to two, before three straight two-out singles and a wild pitch tied the game, setting the stage for an unlikely sequence of events that would emerge as one of the Game's iconic moments— and here I deliberately capitalize the *G* in *Game* to refer not to this one Game 6 but to the game of baseball itself.

To this day, Red Sox fans remember the excruciating, slowly unfolding scene as a dribbler half scooted through the legs of Boston's hobbled first baseman Bill Buckner and into right field, allowing Ray Knight to score from second with the winning run. The picture was particularly painful, alas, because the beloved Sox had been so famously disappointed for so long—a history of frustration and doggedness that has only been partially erased by the franchise's recent run of World Series successes.

Mets fans carry the picture of a joyous Mookie Wilson, the fleet-footed center fielder who'd hit the dribbler and smiled on our legacy, bounding toward first base like a kid who'd been let out of school early and wanted to make it through the front doors before the principal called him back inside.

In my house, ever after, the memory was attached to Vin Scully's iconic call, which I'd taken the time to teach my baseball-mad son Jordan back in 2000, when he was just a kid. To this day, he can recite it word-for-word, cadence-for-cadence: *a little roller up along first . . . behind the bag! . . . it gets through Buckner! . . . here comes Knight! . . . and the Mets win it!* And in Jordan's enthusiasm there was also my own—an astonishment that only seemed to deepen with the years, as we took turns reveling in the game's unlikely turn.

Baseball fans in general flash back on a careening roller-coaster ride that came to symbolize the emotional highs and lows of postseason play. For many, this one play fairly defined the 1986 World Series. Indeed, many will tell you it *decided* the series, which of course was hardly the case. There was still another game to be played.

Game 7—*the deciding game.*

And, as it turned out, I would get the start.

What happens when the stuff of your dreams is at hand? Do you rise to the occasion, step to it, grab on? Do you dig deep and discover new layers of grit and resolve to see you through? Do you harness your talents and have at it? Or do you shrink from the moment and wonder what might have been?

I grew up in Millbury, Massachusetts, just outside Worcester, in a sports-crazed family, with three brothers. Let the record show, I was born in Hawaii, but I was raised in the hardworking, hard-cheering heart of New England. We lived and died with our Boston teams. Their victories became ours—their losses, ours as well. We filled our days with imagined moments of triumph, greatness, transcendence. Always, these moments had to do with snatching victory from the clutches of defeat, finding glory in the specter of gloom. Always, it was about hitting a buzzer-beater shot or a walk-off home run (before the terms were even coined!) or trying to trip each other in the crease with the game on the line—à la Barclay Plager and Robert Gordon Orr. (Gump Worsley never had a chance.)

Game 7 of the 1986 World Series was my *be careful what you wish for* moment—and my heart climbed into my throat as Ray Knight came around to score on the back of that crazy play down the first-base line. It was thrilling and terrifying, both. Understand, it was a glorious team moment, an unlikely, unwieldy rally that lifted us from the ash heap of World Series wannabes and kept us in the running—an exultant, collaborative victory all around. But as my guys went nuts in celebration, as Shea Stadium rocked in mass pandemonium, as long-suffering Mets fans across the New York metropolitan area jumped up and down in shock and awe and *dumbstruckedness,* I held back, because I knew that all of that positive energy would now flow back to me.

I should note here that one of the reasons I held back was because I wasn't in the dugout as these unlikely moments unfolded. For a time, I wasn't even in the ballpark—as I will explain in the pages ahead. But by the time Ray Knight went barreling down that third-base line, by the time Red Sox fans had filled the air with every known expletive (and, undoubtedly, with a whole bunch of new ones, too), I was huddled over a small television screen in the clubhouse (rabbit-eared, in romantic memory), not quite sure how to process what I was seeing. Whatever was happening out there on the field, *however* it was happening, it meant the series would now rest on my arm, in my head.

On my shoulders . . . that's the tired sports cliché that told me the weight of this one win might have been the city's to celebrate but it was mine to carry. Frankly, I didn't do such a good job of it, and I've had half a lifetime to figure out why. I don't set this out in a tough-luck sort of way—that's not my thing. But what *is* my thing is reassessing, reevaluating, revisiting my performance on the field, the same way I now do for other players when I'm calling a game in the broadcast booth, only with me I tend to be a little harder on myself in my analysis than I am on any of today's players.

So what went wrong on that crisp-cool October night in Shea Stadium? A night that, by the lights of my boyhood dreams, should have been the highlight of my baseball career? Well, I'll try to answer that as I take a look at the game, pitch-by-pitch, ache-by-ache, but for now I believe it's helpful to think about the mind-set I carried onto the field that night—a mind-set I carried for the whole of my career. Best way to describe it is a line of thought pinched from a good friend, who back around this time went for an interview for a bond-trading position with a top Wall Street firm. My buddy reported that the interview had gone well. He'd answered all the standard questions in the standard way. He'd hit the highlights of his story—his mom was a teacher, his dad a mail-carrier—and somehow he'd worked his way through Wharton and built an impressive résumé. But in the end he didn't get the job. The Wall Streeters hadn't exactly asked him any tough questions, so he pressed them on it, said it would be helpful to know what he might have missed so he could get it right the next time. Finally, he was told that he'd come from a place of blue-collar dreams. This one firm, my friend was told, wasn't much interested in that type of thinking—for the one-percenters of the day, nothing less than a white-collar mind-set would do.

In time, this term and the thinking behind it have come to explain my falling short in Game 7 and the cap on my career—to me, anyway. And now, all these years later, here's my take: I was *good enough to dream,* to borrow a phrase from the sportswriter Roger Kahn. I was good enough to be recruited by the baseball and football coaches at Yale, good enough to make it to the bigs, good enough to make it to this Game 7. This, alone, was something to celebrate—but this was where it ended for me. Why? Because, at bottom, I was a blue-collar kid. Because there was a limit to my dreaming.

This cap on my thinking was brought home for me in a compelling way by the great slugger Richie Allen, who was working as a coach for the Texas Rangers during my first spring training with the team. (The rest of the baseball world had taken to calling the former slugger Dick Allen, but I knew him as Richie—that's how he introduced himself to me.) I was fresh out of Yale, my head filled with possibilities—with no room in those nooks and crannies for the harsh realities of the game, not just yet. I had it in mind that if I pitched well I could earn a spot in the rotation, but Richie Allen set me straight. He spent a lot of time with me that spring, helped me to see how ugly and tough it was to be a black ballplayer in the '60s and '70s—and, still, how ugly and tough it could be for a young ballplayer looking to crack an Opening Day roster. Remember, this was a guy who'd had a big impact on the game—he was the National League Rookie of the Year in 1964 and the American League Most Valuable Player in 1972, so he'd clearly made his mark. But the game left its mark on him, too, and by the time I met him in 1982, he came across as this beautifully angry individual who'd put the game in its place. He was the first person I met in baseball who gave it to me straight.

He said, "So what is it you'd like to take out of spring training here, youngster?"

(Yep—he called me *youngster*.)

I said, "Mr. Allen, I'd like to win the fifth spot in the rotation."

(Yep—I called him *Mr. Allen*.)

He looked at me and laughed. It took me down a couple of pegs, after I'd put it out there that I thought I had a shot to make the team, but at the same time I couldn't help but join in. He was laughing so hard, I started laughing, too. Finally he said, "Motherfucker, Jon Matlack is making over a half million dollars. You, you're making nothing."

Jon Matlack, in the great circle of baseball life, was part of that legendary New York Mets pitching staff in the early 1970s, and now he was finishing out his career with the Texas Rangers. He had a guaranteed contract. Me, I had no such thing, and Richie Allen had the economics of the game all figured out. He knew I could have had a lights-out spring training, I could have blown everyone away, and there wasn't a chance in Arlington, Texas, that I would make it to the bigs. He laughed and laughed and said, "They're gonna ship your ass to Triple A, brother. Just you wait and see."

But all of that was a lifetime away. As a kid, my blue-collar dreams were still taking shape. Goofing around with my brothers in the backyard, I could see myself sink the winning putt at the U.S. Open. I could serve an ace in my head to end a fifth-set tiebreaker at Wimbledon. I could close my eyes and throw a last-second Hail Mary pass in the Super Bowl. But to achieve greatness, of course, you need to reach for something bigger than pulling out the win at the last possible moment. Absolutely, you need to connect on that desperation touchdown pass, but you also need to throw for 400 yards before going into your two-minute drill. No question, you've got to hit that last-second shot to win the ABA championship (with me, as a kid, it was all about the ABA), but not before you put 50 points up on the board to keep your team in the game. You need to *get* to Wimbledon, to the Super Bowl, to the World Series—and to do *that* you need to visualize a sustained and lasting greatness and not just focus on a fleeting victory.

My dreams were too small, I guess. I didn't go into this Game 7 telling myself, *Okay, I'm gonna stick it to these guys. I'm gonna throw a three-hitter tonight. I'm gonna shut them down and get it done.* I was content to continue my fine pitching performance in the series, without really stopping to consider that *fine* might not cut it. See, for the whole of my baseball life, I'd been conditioned to think of the game as a team effort, which it certainly was. But underneath that *team* effort, there should have been a *me* gene on display. That beautiful anger I saw in Richie Allen, back in my first spring training? I could have used some of that. As a major league pitcher, you need to bring a certain arrogance with you out to the mound, a certain selfishness, and I guess I didn't have that in me—not enough of it, anyway. That swagger, that confidence, that killer instinct . . . I'd been able to get by without these aspects of character on the game's smaller stages. And here I was hoping to do okay, that's all. I didn't want to embarrass myself, my teammates, my family—and that's no way to approach one of these big moments.

I know this now, and I suppose I knew it then, on some level—but I certainly didn't appreciate it. As a young man, well into my major league career by this point, I should have known at least to keep it simple. To think, *Hey, I did a good job against these Red Sox hitters in Game 1 and Game 4. My stuff's better than their stuff. I'm good. We're good.* But that's not how I played it. No, I let the game play me. I let the Red Sox play me, instead of the other way around. My mind drifted. I thought, *This is a veteran team. I've shown them just about everything I've got. I'm gonna have to try something different.*

If I'd had more inner confidence, if I'd had the kind of

arrogant selfishness you see in our greatest athletes, I would have gone into the game thinking I would dictate the at bats. Thinking, *I've owned these guys.* Thinking, *Bring it, Boston!* But my mind didn't go there. Instead, I worried I'd have to come up with a new bag of tricks, else I would be found out.

I hadn't even thrown a pitch and already I was down in the count.

This book is not like other sports books. Certainly, it's not like other books by former ballplayers. Athletes seem to want to write about the times they beat the odds, dominated their opponents, run the table. They write about their victories, just, and if they spend any time at all on their disappointments, it's only to make their victories loom larger still. Nobody writes about the times they've fallen short, but to me that's what's most interesting about this one game, at the butt end of this long, sick, wondrous season.

For whatever reason, I didn't have it that night at Shea, nearly thirty years ago. I'd had a solid year, and my two previous starts in the series had gone well enough, but there was nothing left. I'd written this story a thousand times in my head, but in the end my pitching line told the story instead:

IP	H	R	ER	BB	K
3.2	6	3	3	1	0

As I consider these numbers, I'm torn. I was never the sort of athlete to congratulate myself on a job well done. I was the last person to revel in my accomplishments. Never once did I kick back and think, *Hey, I pitched a great game!* There was always something I could have done differently, something I could have done better, and on this night there were a whole lot of those *somethings*. I don't mean to give away the story just yet, but there are no surprises here: I left the game in the top of the fourth, after hitting Dave Henderson to start the inning, coaxing Spike Owen to fly to right and allowing my opposite number, Bruce Hurst, to sacrifice Henderson to second. We were down 3-0 and it was as if I'd let the air out of the stadium. The contrast between the crowd I left and the crowd that greeted me as I took the mound for my warm-ups was startling. Top of the first, I'd never seen the Shea faithful so pumped. The place was rocking! But it didn't take long for those savvy New York fans to see I wasn't as sharp as I'd been earlier in the series, or for the ruckus to die down on the back of that shared realization. They were still with me in the end—I don't think there was a single *boo* in those 50,032 tightened throats as I left the field—but the few cheers that came my way felt more like pity than appreciation. Those kind enough to cheer felt sorry for me, I think—glad to be rid of me, to be sure, but sorry just the same.

Going in, I worried about my control. I'd walked five Sox batters in Game 4, so it felt to me like these veteran hitters were stalking me, waiting patiently at the plate like the cheetahs I'd watched on those *Mutual of Omaha Wild Kingdom* shows as a kid. Just lurking in the batter's box, ready to pounce the moment I left the ball up in the strike zone, as if they were calling me out.

Even the elements messed with my head. We'd had all kinds of momentum, coming off that come-from-behind, extra-inning win in Game 6, but after a rainout on Sunday night,

October 26, that momentum had leaked away. That extra day allowed the Red Sox to breathe and regroup, leaving me and my Mets teammates with a little too much time to consider how close we'd come to calling it a season.

Advantage: Boston.

And here's another thing: the way we'd come from out of nowhere to win Game 6, the way the Red Sox collapsed when the game was in their grasp, it left a lot of people in our clubhouse thinking we were somehow meant to win this World Series. I didn't feel that way—not one bit. But that's a dangerous perspective, if you allow it to take hold.

That extra day left me with all that time to think, and by Monday night, after going through all my pregame rituals a second time, I was a bundle of restless energy—an agitated, unfocused mess. It was a mess of my own making, let's be clear, but there it was, and even though I managed to pitch my way through the first inning allowing only a single to Bill Buckner, I knew this wasn't going to be my night. The ball felt heavy in my hand.

Sure enough, when Dwight Evans and my old high school rival Rich Gedman led off the second with back-to-back home runs, you could see my shoulders sag and my false-swagger slip away. I felt like Charlie Brown out there on that mound—spinning ass-over-teakettle, my jersey torn from my back by the breeze of those balls off the bats of the Red Sox hitters, a KICK ME! sign stitched to where my name was meant to be.

I left the game with my head held low—the picture of defeat. But we were not done just yet. Somehow, as baseball fans will surely recall, my teammates kept battling. Sid Fernandez came on in relief and held the Red Sox scoreless for the next while, allowing us to catch our own few breaths and put Boston's momentum on pause. We tied it in the sixth, and went ahead on a Ray Knight homer to lead off the seventh, and from there we scratched and clawed our way to another few runs and held off a Red Sox rally in the eighth and managed to win 8–5—erasing, for the moment, the sting of my early-innings failure.

Here again, I don't mean to give away the ending, but I'm assuming most baseball fans know the outcome of that game. They know, as I now know, how the sweetness of that World Series victory would surely linger, but for me it became a bitter sweetness. Over time, the *bitter* could never quite detach itself from the *sweet,* leaving me to wonder, over and over, what might have been. Leaving me to think what it meant to dream only blue-collar dreams.

Game 7 of the 1986 World Series stands in my rearview mirror as a grand moment in time. A career-high (we were the World Champions, after all), intertwined with a career-low (because, let's face it, I'd stumbled on that too-large stage). A reminder that even when you're not on your game the game must be played, and that it's how you move forward through these difficult moments that defines you as a player, a teammate, a person.

As Games 7 go, in baseball and in other sports, this one wasn't much. There were no walk-off heroics, like we saw off the bat of the Pirates' Bill Mazeroski in the 1960 series against the Yankees. This wasn't the 1954 Red Wings skating to a 2–1 victory over the Canadians in overtime, or the 1994 Rangers putting the finishing touches on the Canucks in a Game 7 thriller that returned the Stanley Cup to New York for the first time in fifty-four years. There was no Willis Reed, limping onto the court to inspire his Knicks teammates in a Game 7 clash against the Lakers at Madison Square Garden in 1970.

No—*this* Game 7 was not *that*. This was just a seesaw battle between two tired, emotional, history-laden teams, but the enduring significance of this one game was in the strategy, in the gamesmanship, in the stories it left in its wake. It was in the grace notes it provided to a thrilling World Series. It was in the boisterous, celebrated season that led up to it, the epic showdown in the League Championship Series against the Houston Astros that punched our ticket to the World Series, and the frenetic Game 6 that took our Mets off life support and left us to fight another day. It was in the Curse of the Bambino that followed these Red Sox like a cloud—and in the so-called Mets "magic" that had our team and our fans thinking we were "amazing," and telling us "you gotta believe" and leaving us to think we were somehow charmed. It was in the tension-filled chess match between two curious, colorful managers, and in the end-game strategies each put into play.

It was in the lessons it offered to a young, not-too-confident blue-collar player, at the front end of a lifetime in the game.

7

WHO'LL STOP THE RAIN?

After a thrilling, sick-glorious, back-from-the-dead win like the one we'd managed in Game 6, you want to come right out and do it again the next day. You're juiced, jacked, jumping to get back out on the field, and you know the other guys are probably so derailed by their loss they won't have time to focus. They'll want to turn tail, lick their wounds, block the game from memory.

Poker players have a term for how an opponent might play after a particularly bad beat; they'll say he's "on tilt," and here we could only imagine that Bill Buckner and his Red Sox teammates were tilted and slanted so far over they might as well have been floored. Absolutely, Boston was on its heels, and we were on our toes, and it was in our interests to finish off the series as swiftly as possible.

Anyway, I wanted to get on with it. We *all* wanted to get on with it, I think. If it were up to me, we would have played Game 7 on Saturday night, right then and there, as soon as the

ruckus died down after Game 6 and we could put that adrenaline shot of victory to good and immediate use, but that's not
how the schedule was drawn. This was no sandlot affair, with
the prize going to the last guys standing. No, this was the
World Series—our national pastime on full and glorious display. We had to wait until the following evening to build on
all that good momentum, only it started to look like the
weather wouldn't cooperate and we'd have to wait longer still.
Rain was in the air, in the forecast, all around. This alone
wasn't a worry; as a ballplayer, rainouts and rain delays are an
occupational hazard. What concerned me was how to fill the
time between what just happened and what would happen
next—how to get to the top of the first if the top of the first
was a long way away.

We were thoroughbreds, itching to be let out of the gate,
and the starting gun couldn't come soon enough. It left
me thinking of that great Tom Petty line, "The waiting is the
hardest part."

Looking back, and taking a solipsistic view, I have to
think the waiting was especially hard on me. Admittedly, I
was wired a little differently on this from every single one of
my Mets teammates, from every single Mets fan, from anyone
else who might have taken in all of that Game 6 excitement
full-on. Me, I could only experience the dramatic ending of
that game in a sidelong way. I wasn't even in the building
for most of those extra innings, so I'd ridden those ups
and downs at a distance. For a couple of beats in there, I was
on the Grand Central Parkway, headed toward LaGuardia
Airport—that's how out of touch I was with the emotions of
this one game.

I suppose my absence during these late-inning heroics deserves an explanation. You see, in those days, with 50,032 fans shoehorned into Shea Stadium, it could take us up to two hours to get out of the parking lot after a close game. Our pitching coach, Mel Stottlemyre, was well aware of this and thought to use it to our advantage. Nowadays, teams might send a pitcher home early if he's due to start the next day, especially if the game is running long or headed to extra innings. On getaway days, they'll even send the next day's starter ahead before that day's game is under way. But back then this was something new—something *radical,* even—and on this night Mel became one of the earliest proponents of the practice when he found me with the score tied at the end of the eighth inning and told me to go home.

I wasn't expecting this.

Logistically, it made a lot of sense: beat the traffic, avoid the hassle, create this one extra edge over your opponent who might not know the chaos awaiting them outside the stadium. Personally, it left me feeling out of sorts, like I was abandoning my teammates—even though there weren't a whole lot of foreseeable scenarios that would have put me in this game, unless one of our guys got hurt on the base path and we needed a pinch runner. Still, we were down 3-2 in the series, so there was the very real possibility we could let this adrenaline shot of momentum slip away and allow these Red Sox to end our season, and if that happened I'd want to be with my teammates.

Davey Johnson was on board with this strategy—only here, headed into the ninth, our season still very much on the line, it felt a little premature. We'd just come back to tie the game at 3–3, against a shaky Calvin Schiraldi, our former Mets teammate who seemed to want to be anywhere but out there on that Shea Stadium mound at such a critical moment. Rick Aguilera, who'd done a great job for us in the series against Houston and who'd started to show the stuff that would make him one of the game's dominant closers in seasons to come, was coming in to pitch—and, hopefully, shut things down until we could push across the winning run. At least, that was Mel's game plan. Granted, it was just Aggie's second year in the bigs, but we all had a lot of confidence in him. Mel was liking our chances. He liked Aggie's arm, the energy of the crowd . . . the whole deal. It felt to him like we had the game in hand, and he said as much. He walked over to where I was sitting in the dugout and said, "Get your clothes on and go home. We're gonna win this ball game."

So I did as I was told—reluctantly, but dutifully. Like I said, a part of me felt like I was abandoning my teammates. But I was feeling it, same as Mel. I was feeling it, same as the 50,032 wholehearted Mets fans jumping up and down in the stadium, willing us toward the finish line. I hurried out of my uniform and into my street clothes in the time it took for Aggie to retire the side in the top of the ninth.

Rice, Evans, Gedman. *Strikeout, swinging; E6; ground ball double play.* Not exactly one-two-three, but close enough.

I was in my car—a sweet 1966 Mercedes 220, English-drive convertible—pulling away from the players' parking lot as my teammates returned to the dugout. I had the top down. It was eerily quiet outside the stadium as I drove off. It felt like a ghost town a little bit—with a swirl of hot dog and pretzel wrappers instead of tumbleweeds. Between innings, there had been all kinds of ambient stadium noises seeping through the iconic open-air ramps that used to frame that old building, but by the time I'd reached the Grand Central approach, there were only the still, sweet sounds of a late-October night. The roads were empty—because of course the rest of the city was fixed on the game. The car had no radio, so I could only imagine what was going on inside the stadium.

Then, just as I was leaving the grounds, the night grew quieter still. (As if such a thing was possible!) The stadium seemed to heave—or, better, to moan. (As if this, too, was a prospect.) There was a palpable, discernible, unknowable . . . *something*. Tough to notice, but at the same time tough to miss. If you're a lifelong sports fan, you've undoubtedly experienced a similar phenomenon. You're on your way into or out of a stadium, an arena, an athletic facility of any size or stripe, and you can tell right away that something has happened. Something big. Something of moment. Something calling to you in some way. Something that has nothing at all to do with you just yet, and yet you want in on it just the same. In baseball, you don't have to hear the crack of the bat or the roar of the crowd to know the ebb and flow of a game has turned; you can hear it in a kind of communal sigh. You can feel it in your bones. You can *sense* it. In triumph, the lifting of 50,032 hearts, all at once, can change the air currents in a visceral way, an exhilarating way; in despair, the soft fall of those same 50,032 hearts can suck the air from the night sky.

Oh yes, oh yes, oh yes . . . there's a vibe that flows in and out of these big old ballparks that tells us right away that something's going on—better believe it!—and here it found me as I rolled onto the on-ramp, headed back to Manhattan.

Somehow, with no radio, no crack of the bat, no dialing down on the din of the crowd . . . I knew. Somehow, with the top down, the windows all the way open, the roads fairly empty and the concrete jungle surrounding Shea Stadium all but silent . . . I knew. I felt this cosmic tap on my shoulder that seemed to say, "Not so fast, Ronnie."

The game had turned.

Just *how* it had turned, I had no idea—except it was a safe bet it hadn't turned in our favor. If it had, the few drivers on the road would have started honking, flashing their brights, rolling down their windows and hooting and hollering. If it had, the joyous rumble from the stadium would have found its way to me. I would have felt a tap on my shoulder of an entirely different kind. Understand, at just this moment I was already driving away from the stadium on one of those one-way entrance ramps, so there was no turning back without hopping the curb. (Not about to happen in such a classic ride!) I had no choice but to ease on to the Grand Central Parkway and double-back at the first opportunity. Mercifully, fantastically, it only took a few minutes on these deserted roads, but as I was driving it felt like the longest few minutes in recorded human history. I was desperate to know what had happened to let the air out of the stadium as I pulled away, what was happening still.

There was no radio in that sweet old car—this was back in the prehistoric information age, before smartphones. I was riding blind. Was it just that Aggie had given up a hit? Or were we now down another run (or, worse, another *bunch* of runs) and facing elimination? How was I to know?

What had happened, I'd soon learn, was that in the top of the tenth inning, Boston center fielder Dave Henderson led off with a home run down the left-field line. That was the first nail in the Mets' coffin. But then Rick Aguilera managed to settle, striking out shortstop Spike Owen and pitcher Calvin Schiraldi, who hit for himself despite having just pitched two tough innings.

(Looking back at this game, from the perspective of a baseball analyst, I've always wondered about this decision by Boston manager John McNamara. You'd think a guy like this, a spot like this, the percentage move would have been to hit for the pitcher and throw out a fresh arm in the bottom of the inning.)

Next, Wade Boggs stroked a double to left-center and came around to score on a single by the hot-hitting Marty Barrett, the Red Sox second baseman. Another nail, and we were as good as done.

But I didn't know any of this at the time. I only knew that my teammates were up against it—and I only knew *that* because of all that heaving and moaning coming from Shea. Within minutes, I had pulled around on the opposite side of the stadium from the players' entrance, in front of the old Diamond Club. I left the car at the curb with one of the security guys and dashed inside, like a scene out of a bad romantic comedy where the guy races to the airport to catch the girl before she boards her flight. Through the Diamond Club entrance, there was a back door to the clubhouse. It wasn't our usual route; you had to walk through a grand entryway dotted with framed photos and team memorabilia, and then through another waiting area where club officials often met with visiting league executives and other dignitaries. Then you'd walk through another door past the trainer's room, the doctor's room, and the clubhouse attendant's room.

In those days, our clubhouse attendant was a guy named Charlie Samuels, and he was surprised to see me, just then, out of uniform. I wouldn't say he was *happy* to see me, just surprised.

Mets fans will recognize Charlie's name, of course—he was with the team for over thirty years, but he left the organization in 2010 with his head hung low. He ended up pleading guilty to stealing bats, balls, bases, jerseys, and other memorabilia said to be worth millions of dollars, all told—and as part of his plea deal he was banned from Mets games for life. But back in 1986 we just knew him as part of our extended Mets family. He was about the same age as a lot of the younger players, and a fixture in and around our clubhouse, and when I raced past his office that night he was watching the game on a small nine-inch television screen.

In those days, we all called Charlie "The Fig" after the pear-shaped actor in a Fig Newton commercial that was popular at the time. The Fig looked up from the set as I crossed the threshold of his office and said, "R.J., they scored two in the tenth." Like he was telling me there'd been a death in the family.

My heart sank. I'd expected the worst—and here it was, the worst. I couldn't think what to say, so I just said, "Fuck!" To myself. To Charlie. To the baseball gods that had apparently let us down.

I leaned in close to get a good look at the screen. Just as Charlie was filling me in, I heard a door slam on the other side of the locker room. I heard what sounded like a chair being kicked over. Then I heard the unmistakable voice of Keith Hernandez, who also couldn't think what to say: "Fuck!"

Keith had just flied out to deep center field for the second out of the inning, and had stormed from the dugout in a fit of resignation and frustration, settling into Davey Johnson's office with Darrell Johnson, a baseball lifer who was now a roving scout for the Mets. Check out these loose threads from a life in the game: Darrell Johnson was the Boston manager in 1975 when those Red Sox came back to win a dramatic Game 6 against the Reds, only to lose in Game 7, and here it seemed his new team was about to take him on the same sad roller coaster.

By now I'd put two and two together. We were trailing by those two backbreaking, heartbreaking runs. Bottom of the tenth. Two men out. Down to our last swings of what was supposed to have been "our" season. We'd been strutting and swaggering through these games since spring training as if a world championship was our birthright, and here we were about to be denied.

Gary Carter stepped to the plate, kicked the dirt from his cleats. The Shea faithful stood in a stunned, desperate vigil—biting their shirts, their jackets, their lips. "The Kid," our future Hall of Fame catcher, had fairly struggled this series (despite a Game 4 for the ages!), but there weren't too many guys you'd rather see up in this spot. He was keyed in, determined. And sure enough, he jumped on a 2-1 Schiraldi fastball and ripped a line drive single into short left field.

A heartbeat!

I had thought of crossing the clubhouse to take in these final moments with Keith, one of my closest friends on the team, but there's a tradition in baseball that you don't mess with a good thing. When the stars align and smile on your efforts, you do what you can to keep those stars in place, so as soon as Carter got his hit Keith wasn't moving, and I wasn't moving. There might have been some hits in our seats. Whatever happened next, I'd watch it from that tiny television screen in Charlie Samuels's office. You had to really lean in to that sucker to see what was going on, but I was staying put.

So that's how I took in those wild-ride moments in the bottom of the tenth inning.

Kevin Mitchell, pinch-hitting for Rick Aguilera, pushing Gary Carter to second with a single to center.

Ray Knight, scoring Carter from second with a line drive single to right-center.

Bob Stanley finally coming in for the overmatched, overwhelmed Schiraldi, allowing Mitchell to score the tying run from third on a wild pitch as Knight advanced to second.

Mookie Wilson, hitting that now-famous dribbler down the first-base line that managed to skip between Bill Buckner's legs and into right field, as Ray Knight bounded around third and came home to score, his arms flapping the whole way, like he was about to take flight.

And me, the whole time, leaned in super-close to the screen, shoulder to shoulder with Charlie Samuels, afraid to move a muscle for fear I'd upend whatever mojo my teammates had working out there on the field, in the dugout, wherever.

There was a lot of jumping up and down after that, as you might imagine. In Charlie's office. In Davey Johnson's office. The guys were carried into the clubhouse on a wave of bedlam. I never had a chance to set foot outside, but I could feel every thump and creak and rattle in those old Shea bones. I've been through a couple of earthquakes in my time, and this was right up there. You could actually feel the stadium swaying, see the cement moving on the clubhouse ceiling, choke on the puffs of dust spitting from the popcorn tiles. It was madness, just madness. It really felt for a few moments like that whole place could come tumbling down, and the weird thing about it was that this was not a particularly terrifying thought. I don't recall feeling afraid, or thinking maybe we should get out of there before things got too crazy. No, my only thought was that if you had to go, if this was our time, it was a helluva way to go.

We were untouchable, invincible, after all.

For all of Mel Stottlemyre's concern about getting me home at a decent hour, we didn't get out of that clubhouse until about one o'clock in the morning. I went home to a full house at about two. I had my family staying with me for this run of games, so things were crazy-hectic in my apartment. My brother Brian lived in the building, so he was in his own apartment, but everyone else was staying with me. I had a small two-bedroom, and the rooms were tiny. The closets were tiny, the kitchen was tiny . . . it's like the whole place was done in miniature. My youngest brother Charlie had to sleep on the couch, that's how jammed in we were.

Everyone was wired from the way the game had ended. It felt a little like we'd been given an eleventh-hour reprieve by the governor. We weren't exactly celebrating, because there was nothing to celebrate just yet, but there was a lot of excitement. We were punch-drunk, giddy, and way too pumped to settle down just yet, so it took awhile for my apartment to quiet. There was a lot of unwinding, decompressing, fresh reminiscing we had to get past. At about three-thirty, my father finally took me aside and told me he thought I should try to get some sleep, reminded me that I had a big game the next day, same way he used to see that I got my rest back in Little League.

(Those Little League memories would keep finding me during this series. Here's another one: my father worked as a foreman in a machine shop, and he was always reeking of oil and grease from work, and I remember feeling an enormous sense of pride whenever he came down to the field for one of our practices that he wasn't dressed in a suit like some of the other dads—no "Mad Men" in our family. I guess this was the source of my blue-collar dreams, huh?)

I managed to get in about five hours, but I was restless, fidgety. Mostly I tossed and turned and stared at the ceiling. At some point, I decided a good night's sleep wasn't necessary—a decision I came to by degrees because it just wasn't happening.

All of which takes us back to the rain.

I got out of bed early the next morning, not exactly refreshed, but ready to pitch my ass off. I told myself that it was my arm that needed resting, not the rest of me, and since it had been three days since my last start I was good to go. But then I looked out the window and the reality of the day kicked in. It was a cold, wet morning, the glass flecked with streaks of rain. I switched on the radio to listen to the forecast, and as the weather guy called for rain, rain, rain, I reminded myself that things don't always go the way they're meant to go, on the field and off. You've got no choice but to roll with it, make the best of it, try to turn whatever you're facing into some kind of advantage—while guys on the other team are going through the same motions, doing their own version of the same thing.

Let's not forget, rainouts were not uncommon in my day. Fields didn't drain as well as they do today. Plus, we didn't have such easy access to Doppler radar and other satellite technologies to help us take full advantage of weather windows and patterns. We were at the mercy of the skies, but in the postseason we knew league and network officials would wait out the weather as long as it made sense, which made the waiting tougher still.

Too, we moved about on a kind of knife-edge—more and more, as we went deeper and deeper into the series. To a man, I suspect, we were afraid to drift from our routines and into the unfamiliar, and a rain delay or a rainout or some other snafu could only set us off our game at a time in the season when our routines mattered most of all.

Another thing: John McNamara had announced Dennis "Oil Can" Boyd as his Game 7 starter, and we'd hit Boyd hard in his Game 3 start at Fenway. Nothing against Oil Can, who'd put up some decent numbers that season, but we liked that matchup. With another day of rest, we all knew, McNamara would likely switch gears and bring back Bruce Hurst to start, and Hurstie had us figured. There's an old line in sports that says you want to face your competition at their best, at full strength, but this was one instance where the cliché didn't hold. Of course we'd rather face the guy we'd owned over the guy who'd owned us, so here was another reason we wanted to get the game in as scheduled.

I moved about my cramped apartment and tried not to think about the prospect of rain, but as I looked out the window my mind ran back to 1975 and that classic Game 6 matchup between Boston and Cincinnati that nearly turned on Carlton Fisk's dramatic home run in the bottom of the twelfth inning—a game that had arguably just been supplanted by our own Game 6 as the greatest World Series game of all time, a game that had put Darrell Johnson in the manager's office with Keith Hernandez feeling like one of Yogi Berra's malapropisms: "It's déjà vu all over again." *That* Game 6 was a long time in coming, as the Reds and Red Sox waited out three days of rain before the game was finally played—an unbearably, nail-bitingly long stretch when you're a baseball-mad teenager and your team is down three games to two and facing elimination.

As a young fan, those three days were agonizing. As a player, scheduled to start on this cold, wet day, I couldn't let myself think about waiting even twenty-four hours, so I put the rain out of my mind. After all, it was out of my control; it could rain all day and I'd have to go through these same motions again tomorrow. Or, the skies could clear and I'd have to take the mound as planned—in less-than-ideal conditions. Naturally, I thought about it, but at the same time I tried not to think about it; that whole morning, I played these mind games to a stalemate and prepared as if the game would go off as scheduled. I went through my morning rituals, went into my familiar pregame zone. For example, before a night game, I'd always eat the same lunch—steak, mashed potatoes, peas. A hungry-man type meal to feed the beast raging within. I'd drink a ton of water, especially in the heat of the season. I'd dress to head out to the ballpark, usually at the same time.

Whatever I did, however I lined up my day, I told myself

my behavior fell just short of superstitious. I liked things just so. Like a lot of starting pitchers, I could be somewhat surly on days I was scheduled to pitch. I'd try not to talk to anyone, kept my interactions to a minimum. With a full house in my small apartment, this wasn't so easy, but my family knew to steer clear. I think my dad sat with me as I took my lunch, but he didn't eat anything, didn't say much. There was a lot of walking on eggshells, as I recall. Everyone was careful not to set me off.

Early on in my career, when I was in the habit of taking the 7 train to Flushing, I tried to keep to myself on game days, but there were always fans wanting to talk to me. I could be a bear and piss them off, or I could suck it up and play nice, and as far as I was concerned neither was a good option. The former, I didn't like how I came across; the latter, I didn't like that I was pulled from my thoughts. Sometimes people would talk to me on the train—not because they were baseball fans or had any idea who I was, but just to make conversation. Normally, this is a good and welcome thing, but starting pitchers aren't always in the same neighborhood as *normal*. I was like the guy in that old *Saturday Night Live* skit, where two characters are sitting next to each other on the subway, trying not to make eye contact; finally, their eyes meet and one guy says to the other, "What the hell are *you* looking at?" That was me on game days. It got to where I had to change my commuting strategy, so midway through my second season I started driving to the stadium and I was at least able to vent and fume and glare at the other drivers on the Grand Central Parkway with a degree of anonymity. I could tune out the rest of the world, zone out, work my way through that day's lineup in my head.

Somewhere along the way, I started carpooling with my friend Tony Ferrara, the New York Mets batting practice pitcher. Tony was a sweetheart of a guy, a real character, with one of the best gigs in the game. He pitched batting practice for the Mets *and* the Yankees, and it worked out great because the two teams were never in town at the same time. He also did a lot of baseball-type consulting for movies and television, and even appeared as the third-base coach in the movie *The Natural*. He'd been an actor, a model, a knock-around ball-player, and he was famous in our clubhouse for the way he kept track of all the pitches he'd thrown in batting practice—a running count going back years and years.

Tony and I got along great, so we decided to drive to the stadium together. In the beginning, we drove in Tony's compact Honda Civic. We folded ourselves inside and tried not to kiss our knees jammed against the dashboard if we stopped short. We called that car the Orange Crush, and it was an ongoing conversation during the season, trying to figure out where the thing was parked. Tony wouldn't stay for the whole game, so I'd make my way home on my own, and I'd have to call him the next afternoon and say, "Where's the Crush?"

(These days, I imagine, there'd be an app for this sort of thing.)

We took turns driving. On game days especially, it was nice to sit in the passenger seat and let Tony deal with the hassles of traffic. He knew I liked to be left alone, so we were mostly quiet on the short drive out to the stadium. He'd pick me up on the corner down the street from my apartment—Thirty-third Street and Third Avenue, a location that gave me the opportunity to practice my *New Yawk* accent ("Toity-toid and Toid!"). Then we'd head out to Queens. If we timed it right, we could get to Shea in about a half hour.

From time to time, our carpool would grow to include *New York Times* sportswriter Ira Berkow, and somehow it worked out that I drove Ira to the stadium that Sunday afternoon, in my English-drive Mercedes. Ira had the idea to get a column out of it, and it ran in the paper the next day. The whole way to the stadium, he pushed me to reflect on what this game might mean, how I was dealing with the pressure, all of that, so right away I was out of my comfort zone, forced to interact in a way that went against my pregame nature.

"Is this the biggest day of my life?" Ira quoted me as saying, answering his question with a question as I drove through the rain on the Long Island Expressway. "I'd say no. I hope it's not. It's the biggest day of my baseball career, yes. My getting married was really a special day. And maybe the biggest day of my life was getting accepted to Yale. I remember I had been accepted to Amherst, and I had set my mind that if I don't get into Yale, well, that's okay. But I got the acceptance and it took me two minutes to decide."

Ira went on to write about my father, who'd gotten up at 4:30 every morning, and prompted me to reflect on the stresses of feeding a family of six on a machinist's salary. "That's pressure, too," I said. "I'm not sure if it's any more than pitching in the big leagues, or pitching the seventh game of the World Series. It's just that more people are watching me."

Yes, more people would be watching me—but not just yet.

When we pulled into the players' parking lot at Shea, the rain was coming down hard. The puddles were too big, too deep to dance around or step over, and as soon as I arrived in the club-house I could tell the game would be called. There was a pall over the room. Nobody was getting dressed, because it was clear that Major League Baseball was waiting to pull the plug. You could just tell—only, this big a game, on this big a stage, there were probably a couple of thousand people who had to sign off on the decision, so we were left to sit and fidget. Nobody could tell us what was going on.

In the meantime, I had to do a press conference. This took me by surprise, set me off. Jay Horwitz came up to me in front of my locker and told me I was expected in the press room. I was already wired pretty tight, my usual surly game day self, and it's possible I poured the surly on extra-thick, playing catch-up since I'd had to spend all that time with Ira in the car on my best behavior. I lit into Jay, the Mets press secretary—one of the game's good guys. I'd done a presser the day before, heading into Game 6, when I had to make myself available to answer the usual questions about a potential start in Game 7. *Yes, I'm ready. Yes, I feel great. Yes, I'm fine on just three days' rest. . . .* To have to go through these same motions the very next day struck me as absurd. And I said as much to Jay, told him I thought it was bullshit.

Bullshit or no, these pressers came with the territory—so here again, as ever, I did as I was told. I was the first to face the gauntlet, and I gave another bunch of same-seeming answers to another bunch of same-seeming questions. It's as though I was on autopilot, not really thinking. But then something happened. As I was walking out of the press room, I passed Dwight Evans and Don Baylor on their way in—only I didn't recognize them straightaway. It always threw me, seeing guys on the other team out of uniform, dressed in their regular clothes; there was a weird disconnect with how I pictured them as opponents and how they moved about away from the game. Don Baylor had no such trouble recognizing me, and he made a good-hearted attempt at small talk. He said, "Hey, Ronnie, what's going on?"

We'd never met, but he couldn't have been friendlier, more professional. It was a class move, on his part. And yet for whatever reason, I could only manage a grunt or a shrug in return—a no-class move, but I didn't think anything of it until years later when Baylor wrote a book and called me out on this.

Baylor would go on to appear in the 1987 World Series with the Minnesota Twins, and the 1988 series with the Oakland A's, making him the only player in baseball history to appear in three consecutive World Series with three different teams, but at the time I only cared that he was a force in the middle of that Red Sox lineup. Evans, too, was a bona fide star at that stage of his career, while I was a relative pissant who'd only been in the game a couple of years.

Also, in my defense, I was a skittish kid—overly respectful of my place in the baseball pecking order. In my day, opposing batters didn't really fraternize with pitchers, even at neutral events like the All-Star game—it just wasn't done. So here *my* sense of decorum was not *their* sense of decorum on this wet afternoon. I hadn't meant to disrespect these two great players, but of course they took my behavior as a kind of snub. Without realizing it, without meaning to, I'd given them an edge, as they went through their own pregame rituals. I'd left the door open for them to think, *Fuck this guy. Who the hell does he think he is, blowing us off like that?* As if I needed to give them any more reasons to want to knock me out of the game.

The press conference itself was wearying, draining. It's one thing to prepare for a game in your head, but to have to do so in front of the media takes it to a whole other level. To have to set your focus aside, it's a distraction. It wears you out—that is, it *can* wear you out, if you let the pressures of the situation seep in. Regrettably, I did just that, but in my defense this was the fifth time in twelve days that I'd been put through these paces. During the playoffs (back before it was called the League Championship Series), I'd been tapped to be the Game 7 starter against the Houston Astros, so I had to face this same press gauntlet, these same questions: *Yes, I'm ready. Yes, I feel great. Yes, I'm fine on just three days' rest. . . .* We ended up winning that series in six, following a sixteen-inning grind at the Astrodome, so my start was pushed back to Game 1 of the World Series, whereupon we went through these same motions again. Add another go-round before Game 4, and these two dog and pony shows before Game 7, and I was fresh out of platitudes and pontifications. How much was there to say about these meaningful games? How many times could I answer the same questions? How much energy could I bring to these sessions without sucking a corresponding amount from my game?

Nothing much had changed when I got back to my locker. Guys were still milling around, waiting on word. Some of my teammates were taking treatments, some were half dressed in uniform, some were still in their civilian clothes. Whatever looseness and confidence we'd felt the night before, immediately following the game, had been washed away by the rain, by these strange, strained circumstances. We were all variously out of sorts. In my case, I was feeling particularly drained, spent—that's how far removed I was from my routines. My visiting family, the rain, the chatty car ride with Ira Berkow, the umpteenth press conference . . . it all added up to where I was now counting on this looming rainout.

My arm felt great, the short rest would not have been an issue, but my head was out of the game.

At long last, the game was called. There was no big announcement. No team meeting. No hands-in chant of "Mets on three!" Davey Johnson didn't gather his players and tell us what time to report the next day, tell us to get a good night's sleep. No. There was just a whispering wave that seemed to wash over the clubhouse, and we all kind of knew—another cosmic tap on the shoulder that told us what was what. Someone went to the chalkboard in the center of the room and wrote down the time we needed to report the next day—four-thirty, for an eight o'clock game. Another someone started putting away a bunch of food that had been left out.

We couldn't get out of there fast enough. We were all out of our element, all of us anxious to ease back into our routines and try again tomorrow. As far as I knew, everybody went off in their own directions. I suppose it's possible a couple of guys paired off and went for a bite to eat, but there was no group outing, no night on the town. We might have been cutups during the regular season, and closed our share of bars and nightclubs, but here in the postseason we were all business. (Or, I should say, we were *mostly* all business.) Me, I went back to Manhattan—this time without Ira Berkow for company. This time, I would keep to myself, as I should have done on the way out to the stadium.

I didn't go straight to my apartment—although, probably, this would have been the veteran move. But I wasn't a veteran quite yet. Plus, I had my family staying with me, and we had to think about dinner, so I called ahead before leaving Shea, told them to stay put, told them the game had been postponed, and suggested we all meet at Pino's, a terrific Italian restaurant in my neighborhood.

Pino's was run by a guy named Jerry Casale, who used to pitch for the Red Sox. Jerry was from Brooklyn originally and I was a fish-out-of-water kid from New England, and he kind of took me in and showed me the ropes. Plus, his food was tremendous. I took a lot of my meals there—even after I got married, I'd find my way to Jerry's place. I'd always go by myself and sit in the back at the worst table, right next to the kitchen, and Jerry would sit down and we'd talk baseball, or Brooklyn, or bruschetta. It was a real family operation; Jerry had his wife working the front, his daughters working the tables, his brother cutting the meat downstairs, and he made his regulars feel like family, too. One of his favorite things, if he'd had enough to drink, was to dust off this old reel-to-reel footage he kept of his one shining moment with the bat, when he hit a home run in a Red Sox uniform at Yankee Stadium. He always said it was the highlight of his career—his greatest hit!—and to watch him relive that moment in the dark of his restaurant, listening to Phil Rizzuto's "Holy Cow!" color commentary, was one of the delightful kicks of my early career.

I wasn't the only ballplayer to hang out at Pino's. Once,

I walked in and saw Mickey Mantle, Whitey Ford, and Billy Martin huddled at a table toward the back. I was afraid to say anything because, hey, this was Mickey Mantle, Whitey Ford, and Billy Martin, and I was just a green, wide-eyed kid in my second year in the bigs. So I nodded in their direction, gave them the respect they deserved, and moved to my regular crappy table. They knew who I was, apparently, because one of them called out to me: "Hey, rook! Whatchya doing?"

I shrugged, said I was just sitting down for a quick dinner.

At this, another one of these greats kicked out an empty chair at their table, said, "Sit down, rook."

For the next couple of hours, I sat and listened to these giants of the game. I didn't say much, unless one of them asked me a direct question. "Where you from, kid?" "How do you like the Yanks this year, kid?" Mostly, they just swapped stories— stories I'll stop just short of repeating out of respect for the families of these great ballplayers.

At the shank of the evening, these three great friends stood, as if on cue, and made their good-byes. Naturally, they stuck me with the bill, which is how it goes when old ballplayers pal around with us youngsters. Still, it was an astonishing thing. What was astonishing was not that these guys would duck out on their tab, but the *size* and *scope* of that tab was just about headline-making: thirty-six 7 and 7s. Thirty-six! Do the math—that works out to twelve drinks each, and what was also astonishing was that the three of them hadn't seemed drunk at all. (Okay, maybe they were *a little bit* drunk, but they weren't tripping over one another or slurring their words.)

The bill came to just under $300. In those days, I had

maybe $400 in my checking account, so I sidled up to Jerry Casale and handed him the bill a little sheepishly.

I said, "Jerry, I'm so sorry, but I don't have this kind of money on me."

Jerry took the check, tore it up, and let rip a full, throaty laugh. "Those guys," he said, meaning Mantle, Martin, and Ford. "They never pay for their drinks."

(This would have been good to know, before I started moving all that money around in my head, trying to figure out a way to cover their tab—and just so you know, they didn't pay for their dinner, either.)

Pino's was like a home away from home, and Jerry was good enough to treat my family like family. He set us up at a big old table and brought out a couple of plates of pasta, some chicken, some broccoli, some salads. We were like his guests of honor that night because, hey, it's not every day you get to host the kid pitcher who's scheduled to start Game 7 of the World Series for the hometown Mets. And, as a kid pitcher with my entire family in tow, it's not every day you get to grab at a moment like this right here—a point of pause in the middle of a great big scrum of attention. At times, at Shea, it felt to me as if the whole world were watching, and yet here at Pino's we might as well have been back home, arguing over the last spoonful of pasta.

It's like the rest of the world fell away.

It wasn't how I would have scripted it, because I was still agitated about the rainout, still worrying about the Red Sox lineup, still locked into my pregame mind-set—and yet as moments go, this one right here was pretty damn great.

2

THE IMPOSSIBLE DREAM

Turns out *pretty damn great* was also *pretty damn personal*. This World Series matchup was the story of my baseball life, writ large. I'd known this on some level going in, and I felt it in a deep-down way when I was in its middle . . . but it becomes even more apparent, looking back.

Baseball touches you in fundamental ways. It does. Your first taste of the game becomes an abiding memory, meaning, the way you're wired as a kid becomes the way you're *hardwired* ever after. A lifelong Cubs fan looks out at the world in a certain way, always hoping for the best while somehow bracing for the worst. A lifelong Yankees fan takes an inverse approach, *expecting* the best and never quite *accepting* anything less. A Cardinals fan, say, might go through life doing just enough to get and keep ahead, in ever-changing ways—and, he'll love his Cardinals players, no matter what.

For the longest time—indeed, for the whole of my growing

up—the lot of the card-carrying Red Sox fan was to fall in line somewhere toward the back. We didn't tempt fate, we accepted it. We were good enough to dream, but not nearly good enough to get it done. Not even close. And we loved our players, too, just not enough to overlook their flaws, their missteps. It was okay for one of us to ride one of our own, but God help the enemy fan who talked trash about our beloved Sox.

Consider: the Red Sox hadn't had a winning season since 1958, hadn't been to the World Series since 1946, hadn't *won* the World Series since 1918, and by the time I came along they were in the cellar. Every year, they'd finished last, or next to last, or damn near next to last; every year, the diehards would drift from the stadium, attendance dropping in lockstep with the Red Sox in the standings—the law of diminishing returns on full display. There were no pink baseball caps dotting the Fenway crowd, the way you'll see today, no full family outings, no Neil Diamond anthems pulsing on the stadium sound system—just a bunch of guys named Sully, swigging a bunch of beers and cheering on their *Sawx*.

In 1965, the first summer I started really following baseball, my hometown team lost 100 games. One hundred games! That's a steep mountain to climb, to be down so low and expect to reach the top, but as a freshly minted fan I was endlessly and innocently hopeful. (Also, I was five and six and seven years old . . . so what the hell did I know?) Oh, there were other teams with long World Series droughts, but the Red Sox I knew back then weren't even competitive beyond the first couple of weeks of April, so it's a wonder I followed the team at all. But I was a kid from Millbury, in a sports-mad household, so of course I followed the team. And frankly, I cared more that they hadn't won last night than they hadn't won in years and years.

The lot of Red Sox fans started to change in the summer of 1967, only they took awhile to spark to it. The home opener at Fenway drew only 8,324—a heartbreakingly small number, especially when you compare it to the throngs that now pack Lansdowne Street before and after every game. But like I said, that all started to change, and by the end of the season the Red Sox would finish first in the league in home attendance. (Hey, how's *that* for a turnaround?) By some wild alchemy, some shift in the prevailing winds of our national pastime, the momentum started to swing our way, mostly on the back of Carl Yastrzemski. More than any other individual player I've ever followed in a team sport, Yaz carried the load. More than any Boston athlete I'd seen play other than Bobby Orr, he lifted a city.

Every morning during the season, my brothers and I would wake and wonder what Yaz had done the night before. It was the burning question of my childhood, and each day I awaited the answer, the same way other kids followed the latest heroics of Superman or Batman. The answer wasn't always close at hand. There were no sports tickers, no ESPN, no talk radio, no way to know at the stroke of a couple of keys the results of any sporting event on the planet as it unfolded. We had to wait until these outcomes found their way to us, and very often they found us in the box scores and game accounts of the morning paper. I had a newspaper route for a while, so I'd get a first look at the sports pages before I set off on my rounds, but that came a little later. As a little guy, I have a clear memory of waking up early and reaching for the morning newspaper to see what happened after one of those great Ali heavyweight bouts, and on pretty much *every* morning following a Red Sox night game during that great stretch run of 1967. In those days, I was usually the first to wake in our house—other than my father, of course, who went to work at 4:30 in the morning, hours before the *Worcester Telegram* was delivered, neatly folded, in our mailbox. I would run outside, grab the paper, and fist it open to the sports pages, careful to preserve the fold so I could restore the thing to its original pristine state. On Sundays, I'd press my father to get the *Globe,* which in those days had some of the best baseball writers to ever cover the game: Leigh Montville, Will McDonough, Peter Gammons, Bob Ryan. They also had a killer Sunday sports section, with expanded stats and extra features. I could get lost in those pages for hours.

At seven years old, I had to go to bed way too early to watch those night games—typically by seven-thirty or eight o'clock, even over the summer. (I think my parents hit on that early bedtime for all four of us kids just so they could squeeze in a precious few hours of peace and quiet and alone time.) I'd fall asleep imaging some new Yaz heroic, some crooked number in the box score next to his name, an exclamation-pointed headline adding to his legend to lead the sports section. I'd wake up and position myself in front of the mirror, trying to perfect my Yaz batting stance—I must have spent half that summer trying to imitate his swing.

For the first time in my life I got caught in the thrill of how important these late-summer games could be. And Yaz, he carried that team on his back—with me along for the ride. If the Sox lost a couple of games on Friday and Saturday, Yaz would come back with that big hit on Sunday to salvage a game in the series and keep his team (*my* team!) in the hunt. The Sox contended all season long and closed to two and a half games back by August, in what was developing as a five-team race for the American League pennant with the White Sox, Tigers, Twins, and Angels. Remember, this was back before the onset of division play and *way* before the establishment of the wild card, so the entire league was scrambling for the top spot—a thrilling season by any measure, but especially so by the measure of a seven-year-old kid who'd never *really* had any reason to root, root, root for his hometown team.

By September, the Red Sox were in first place, and it got to where everyone in New England—everyone in what we now know as Red Sox Nation—was eyeing these late-summer games, biting their fingernails, wondering the same thing my brothers and I had wondered all season long.

What did Yaz do last night?

As most fans of a certain age can recall, Carl Yastrzemski ended up winning the Triple Crown that year, leading the league in batting average, home runs, and runs batted in—a big deal, although to me at the time it was more of an afterthought, a grace note. Recall, Frank Robinson had won the Triple Crown just the year before, so I had no reason to think it would be nearly fifty years before Miguel Cabrera finally earned the next one. To me, just then, a Triple Crown was something that happened from time to time, a natural by-product of a long season, and here it happened that all those hits and homers and runs batted in added up to this glorious pennant race.

That entire summer, whether you were at Lake Winnipesaukee in New Hampshire, on the Cape, in Burlington, Vermont, or a student at Smith College, you were cheering for Carl Yastrzemski, pulling for him to pull his Red Sox teammates across that elusive finish line. And that's just how it felt—like Yaz was pulling the rest of the team along. Every day, he found a way to help them win—to help *us* win. Every day, he spun an extra bit of magic on that field, even on defense, like the time early in the season when he saved a no-hitter against the Yankees for rookie pitcher Billy Rohr with an over-the-shoulder, back-to-the-bases catch in deep left. (Okay, so the no-hitter was later broken up by Elston Howard, who would end the season playing for my beloved Red Sox, who stroked a soft single to right-center with two outs in the ninth—but as heroics go, as *magic* goes, this catch was right up there.)

Every day, we stopped what *we* were doing to see what *he* was doing.

Absolutely, it was the summer of Yaz—at least, in my limited worldview. And, out of that summer, I think I had my first thoughts on what it meant to matter. Like a lot of kids, I wanted to grow up to be a professional athlete—hockey, football, baseball—whatever was in season, that was the dream I was growing. But here, watching Carl Yastrzemski will himself and his teammates through these paces, capturing the full attention of everyone I knew, everyone I cared about . . . this was a lesson on what it meant to be truly great, what it meant to be counted on, what it meant to make a difference.

I became a baseball fan that summer, and once the game got into my blood there was no shaking it. And the Red Sox, they were in there, too, and I mention this deep connection because it must have played with my head as these 1986 World Series games approached. I didn't think so at the time. I would not let it at the time. I was professional about it, analytical about it. My allegiance was with the New York Mets, one hundred percent. My fortunes were tied to the New York Mets, one hundred percent. My focus was on winning a World Series for the New York Mets, one hundred percent. But even as a big-league sapling, now three full seasons into my career, I still scoured the box scores each day during the season to see how the Red Sox were doing—force of habit, I guess. On some level, I was still that seven-year-old kid from the summer of 1967, pulling for Carl Yastrzemski and the Boston Red Sox. The world had changed, of course. *I* had changed. Yaz had given up his spot in left field to a young, quick-wristed slugger from South Carolina named Jim Ed Rice.

But the more things changed, the more they remained the same. These were *my* Red Sox, after all.

Another few words on that 1967 Red Sox team, as long as I'm on 'em . . .

In the end, the pennant came down to a two-game series with the Minnesota Twins at Fenway Park on the last weekend of the season. The Tigers were still in it, too. The Red Sox trailed the Twins by a game in the standings, which meant they'd have to sweep the series, but the Tigers would have to lose at least one game in their series against the Angels, who had fallen out of the race.

Yaz was true to form that weekend, going seven for eight with a home run and six runs batted in, to put the shine on his Triple Crown. That one home run turned out to be key, because Harmon Killebrew of the Twins hit one, too, and the two ended up sharing the American League home run title—good enough to count in the Yastrzemski column as a league-leading effort. Jim Lonborg started the last game of the season and pitched the Red Sox to a 5–3 win for his twenty-second victory. The Tigers, meanwhile, managed to win the first game of a doubleheader, but their bullpen was unable to hold the lead in the second game, giving the Sox their first American League pennant in twenty-one years—and, more importantly, more compellingly, the first in my lifetime.

I can still remember listening to those games on the radio. Curt Gowdy had been the voice of the Red Sox when I started following the team, but he'd been called up to the bigs and was now working for NBC—another great irony of this game, this season, this career, since I now work for Curt Gowdy Jr. at SportsNet New York (SNY), the regional sports network that carries the Mets. Those games were played in my mind for the most part, since we never seemed to have a working television, never could get the reception just right. Still, I had an indelible image of Yaz at the plate, his bat held high, and that's the stance I tried to mimic when I played wiffle ball with my brothers. I was a right-handed hitter, but I couldn't do Yaz justice from the right side of the plate, so I switched to the left and flailed miserably at the ball as it sailed past.

Another thing I remember from that summer was a souvenir record I bought called "The Impossible Dream." That phrase, which was taken from a popular song from the hit Broadway musical *Man of La Mancha,* became a kind of rallying cry for the season. A couple of guys on the team put out a record with that song on it, and like dewy-eyed fans my brothers and I listened to it over and over.

Just to be clear, Yaz had a whole bunch of help in the Boston lineup, although of course he was named Most Valuable Player—an understatement of epic proportions. Tony Conigliaro, who was famously beaned by a pitch from Angels pitcher Jack Hamilton late in the season, and Rico Petrocelli joined him on the All-Star team, along with Jim Lonborg, who also grabbed the Cy Young Award that year. Petrocelli was a particular favorite of mine, because he played shortstop, and in my little-kid head I wanted to be a big-league shortstop, just like him.

(That Conigliaro beaning happened on August 18, 1967, a day before my 7th birthday, and there wasn't a whole lot of celebrating going on in our household that year. We were *all* tore up about Tony C.—me most of all, so of course I refused my mother's traditional birthday cake.)

And—again, just to be clear—that Red Sox team lived up to their rallying cry, because in the end they fell short, losing the World Series to the St. Louis Cardinals in seven games, cheered along by *their* legion of fans who had been schooled in the art of believing just enough in a goal that was just within reach, so my brothers and I slipped bittersweetly into the off-season, dreaming the impossible, still.

But even against that bittersweet, long-suffering backdrop, the competitor in me wanted desperately to face Boston in the 1986 World Series. I wanted to do battle with my hometown team—a chance to make my own impossible dream *possible*. Also, I had a chip on my shoulder. Why? It was a Boston scout who came to one of my games when I was a senior in high school to check me out and set me straight. I've never mentioned his name, and I won't mention it here because I don't want to dishonor this man or his family, but I can share his scouting report. Never mind that it was an accurate take—it wasn't a take I wanted to hear. Understand, anyone who played ball who grew up in the Boston area wanted on some level to play for the Red Sox. I was no exception. So when this scout came up to me after a game, I was over the moon. I knew who he was, of course, but he introduced himself anyway. He said, "Hey, kid, I hear you're going to Yale."

It was a statement pinch-hitting for a question.

I realize now that he was just covering himself with the front office, confirming that I had committed to Yale, that I was not "draft-able." But at the time, all I knew was that he'd cut my legs out from under me, punched me in the stomach.

I answered his non-question with a nod, said, "Yes, sir. I'm going to Yale."

And he said, "That's good, because you'll get a great education. You're a great athlete, kid, but you'll never be a major league baseball player."

And just like that, I was dismissed, reduced . . . *pissed*. To the scout, it was just something to say. To me, it was like another rousing chorus of that song from *Man of La Mancha*. Of course, the man was absolutely correct in his assessment of Ron Darling as a major league prospect. I was a shortstop— *just* a shortstop. I didn't start pitching—*really* pitching—until I got to college. So this guy was spot-on, because I didn't have what it took to be a big-league shortstop. College, maybe, but that was where it would end for me. And now here were these same Red Sox, this same scout still toiling on the team payroll, and me with a whole other something to prove.

Was I torn, to be going up against my beloved Sox? Not really, not hardly . . . and yet, maybe just a little. The points of connection were close enough to touch, in a six-degrees-of-separation kind of way, only here that 1967 team was merely *once* removed from this 1986 version. Remember, toward the end of his Hall of Fame career Carl Yastrzemski had ceded left field to Jim Rice, who still loomed in the heart of the Red Sox batting order, poised to wreck our season. Like his predecessor, Rice could sling the team on his back and carry it forward . . . if the kid pitcher with stars in his eyes would only let him.

If the kid pitcher would take the mound like the child he once was instead of as the champion he was hoping to be.

3

SCOUTING REPORT

And so the rain came and went, and we did it all over again the next day. Same agenda. Same restless night's sleep. Same younger brother crashing on my couch. Same surly attitude. Same lunch. Same commute—this time solo.

The only real difference, as I made my way into the clubhouse, was that this time I was flagged by a Major League Baseball official. Mets General Manager Frank Cashen was with him. Someone said, "Ronnie, there's something we need to talk to you about."

The something they needed to talk to me about was a death threat. Against me. It was put to me in a matter-of-fact way, like someone asking for my autograph. Like it was no big thing. And I guess it wasn't. This sort of thing happened all the time to a lot of ballplayers and people in the public eye, but it was a first for me. I'd had a stalker the year before—a woman who used to show up in my neighborhood at the oddest moments. If I went out for a run early in the morning, there she'd be across the street. If I stepped out to go to dinner, she'd be waiting. If I went to hail a cab, I'd catch a glimpse of her on the corner. This went on throughout the season, sometimes daily, until I finally confronted her, and once I laid it out for this woman, asked her to consider how her behavior appeared, she backed off. So I didn't think anything of it when the Major League Baseball official told me about this death threat. I shrugged it off. It was vague, nonspecific.

I was twenty-six years old, about to take the mound for Game 7 of the 1986 World Series. I was immortal, you know. Nothing could touch me.

Whatever it was, whatever it wasn't . . . I put it out of my mind. It wasn't something to tell my wife, my parents, my brothers. The only way it registered, really, was like a scene from *The Natural,* that great Robert Redford movie based on the Bernard Malamud novel that turned on the attempted murder of Redford's Roy Hobbs character.

(Forgive me, please, this second Malamud reference in this slim volume, but he must have had the Metropolitans in mind when he rolled up his sleeves and started writing. Really, the way we'd come back to win Game 6 was almost supernatural—and now to have to consider the super-creepiness of this death threat—it's like we were all characters in someone else's story.)

I wasn't concerned for my own safety so much as I worried over my routine, my preparation. This was the most important moment of my baseball life, and everything had to fall just right for me to keep on my game. I didn't have time to listen to how the league meant to keep me safe. There would be extra precautions, I was told—and, indeed, if you look at

52

the footage from that night, you can see a bunch of plain-clothes guards up and down our dugout bench. Already there was a beefed-up security presence throughout the stadium and down on the field, but here it was ratcheted up a couple of notches, so I half listened as they walked me through these details.

The nature of the threat was never made clear to me, and I didn't press the issue. I put it out of my mind the moment baseball officials put it in there, because I had it in my head that nothing could touch me, and I only mention it here for context. I want to set the scene, as it spread out before me, and as I set these thoughts to paper now it occurs to me that this feeling of invincibility was connected in some way to how I felt after Game 6, when it felt to me as though the stadium would collapse beneath the weight of that furious celebration. It was something to notice, and then to set aside, and here again I got to thinking, *Hey, if this is my time . . .*

I never asked if any other players had been threatened, because it didn't much matter. I never asked if the threat might have included my family. I just nodded my head and half listened until Jay and the baseball security guy said what they had to say.

"So we're good?" I finally said when everyone had stopped talking.

And we were. Good enough, anyway, for me to turn my full attention to these Boston Red Sox—the only threat I gave a plain shit about just then. A big game like this—big upon big upon big—you go over the other team's lineup like it holds a great secret. A tendency, a weakness, a surprise . . . some way to measure your opponent. But there were no secrets here, on either side of the diamond. This was *exactly* the same Boston lineup I'd faced in Game 1 of the series at Shea Stadium, and *essentially* the same lineup I'd faced in Game 4 at Fenway Park, where the always dangerous Don Baylor grabbed the bat from the hands of pitcher Al Nipper and took his rightful spot in the fat middle of the Red Sox order as the designated hitter.

And me, I was the same pitcher this third time around, only less so.

Here's the thing: as a starting pitcher, there's room up your sleeve for a certain number of tricks, and here I was facing these same professional hitters (on this same grand stage!) for the third time in just ten days. As edges go, this one probably went against me. At best, it did me no favors; at worst, it dug me a hole. Typically, as you work your way through the lineup, you want to hold something back for the later innings. You show your stuff on a need-to-know basis. First at bat, you show as little as you can, as much as you need. Second at bat, you show a little bit more, because you might need a little bit more. By the third at bat, you're putting it all out there, because by now the hitters have adjusted, so you find an extra gear, a different arm angle, a subtle shift in your delivery . . . whatever you've got left, whatever it takes.

This was a tough assignment, and I let myself believe it was a tough assignment, which made it tougher still. This was where that edge came in—and I put it in my head that an edge was key. This was a smart, veteran Red Sox team, shot through with All-Stars, MVP candidates, and future Hall of Famers. Game 1, I think I fooled them. We lost the game 1–0, but I'd pitched well, allowing one unearned run in seven innings. Game 4, I fooled them a little less, but we managed to win this one, 6–2. My pitching line this second time out: another seven innings, with nothing across. It only followed, then, that for this Game 7 I'd have to find a whole bunch of new ways to fool these guys. They weren't about to miss too many mistakes.

In the other dugout, I now imagine, the Boston hitters might have flipped the same line of thought. They might have been thinking this Darling kid had shut them down in those first two games. Maybe they were feeling frustrated, stymied, out of sync. Maybe they would have given the edge to me, on the thinking that I'd frustrated them twice already and that I wasn't about to ease up on this third outing. Or maybe they were thinking they'd seen enough, and had by now made such a careful study of my mechanics that they were brimming with confidence.

Maybe they had my number at last.

But I could only take a narrow, self-absorbed view. This game wasn't about the Boston Red Sox. It wasn't about Bruce Hurst, my opposite number on the hill. It was about me and the New York Mets—but mostly about me. At least, that *should* have been my approach. I *should* have drawn on some of that beautiful anger Richie Allen talked to me about back in my first spring training and swallowed hard and made this game all about me—because it was. Absolutely, it was.

(If only I had known.)

Anyway, who knows what the Red Sox players were thinking? Who knows which side *really* had the edge going in? But I do know this: my biggest mistake was letting my thoughts wander in just this way. As a starting pitcher, the idea is to clear your mind, not clutter it, and here I was caught up in a bunch of doublethink. That said, I believe I did a pretty good job deflecting the death threat against me. I'd set it aside. But this right here was a threat I couldn't quite contain—my mind getting the better of me. If this had been a nothing-special start, on a nothing-special day in August, with nothing much on the line but the long string of the season, I would have taken a different approach. I would have been thinking, *Hey, let me get twenty-seven outs.* Or, *Hey, just give me the damn ball.* There would have been some arrogance to my demeanor, some bluster. But this game was not that. And, clearly, I was not that kind of athlete—not on this night, anyway. My head was not quite where it should have been. About the best I could manage, in terms of mind-set, was, *Hey, I'm gonna go as hard as I can, as long as I can.* That's it—hardly a championship take, hardly enough to see me through. This was Game 7 of the World Series, after all, and here I was leaving the door open to doubt and worry.

And, fear. Not fear that I was in any kind of mortal danger, flowing from that vague death threat. Not fear that, in celebration, this creaky old stadium might come down around us. No. What I was afraid of, really, was that I somehow didn't belong in this spot. That I was in over my head.

This *third start in ten days* business was a part of that. I'd turn on the radio, listen to the reporters in the dugout talking up how the last time a pitcher had made three World Series starts without giving up an earned run, Whitey Ford was posting three straight shutouts for the 1960 and 1961 New York Yankees. Hearing, *no one's ever done this . . . no one's ever done that . . .* I let all that noise mess with my head. I didn't buy into it, not fully, but it was there. I'd let the moment get too big, to where it seeped into my pregame ritual. It's like I'd stepped in shit on my way out to the mound, and I couldn't scrape it off my cleats. Left me thinking, *Oh, this is gonna be a long slog.* Left me thinking I was up against it.

Let's be clear: the best of the best don't allow themselves to think in this way. They don't. Michael Jordan never went into a Game 7 thinking, *I've made a bunch of shots in this series, I sure hope I can make a few more.* No way. He was thinking, *I'm due for sixty tonight.* Or, *This is my time.* Wayne Gretzky never thought, *If I can just manage to skate hard, we can find a way to hang on and win.* No way. If his season was on the line, you can bet he was thinking, *I'll get four assists tonight, and put one in myself.* Or, *Just try to stop me.*

However big the moment, the great ones have a way of harnessing it, riding it, building on it until it becomes bigger still. But this wasn't me, just then. No.

I don't mean to put myself on the same pedestal as athletes like Jordan and Gretzky. And I certainly don't place myself at the level of some of my own teammates from that 1986 New York Mets team—guys like Doc Gooden, Darryl Strawberry, Gary Carter, Keith Hernandez, and on and on. But here I didn't even give myself a chance. Here I was defeated before I'd thrown the first pitch. Why? Because I'd let myself believe it would be a battle instead of a cakewalk. Because I set to wondering which side had the advantage. Because I'd allowed all that talk about this being my third start against this veteran team to set me reeling.

Because I fretted instead of fumed.

Here's another thing: when you take the mound in a

game, you want to be thinking about the first batter, just. That's a winning mentality, a winning approach. One batter at a time, and you set it up in your head so you set them down, one batter at a time. That's how it goes—how it *should* go, like ducks in a shooting gallery. You want to dictate each at bat. But the bigger thought, the overriding thought as I stepped onto that field and walked to my "office" sixty feet and six inches from home plate, was that I'd better not screw up. It was all about hanging in there, hanging tough, hanging on, long enough to give my team a chance to win. I'd made some mistakes in Game 1 and Game 4. I'd gotten away with them, for the most part. And yet I kept thinking about the mistakes I might make here on in, and that's no way to start a game.

Death threat or no, these Red Sox would be gunning for me.

I'd done my homework this third time around. I'd studied the lineup, again and again. The first Boston batter, Wade Boggs, had led the league in hitting that year—the third time in four years. But he had no power. At least, he had no power on display. There was talk, in and around the game, that if he was fooling around in BP, Boggs could hit as many out as anyone else on his team, but like a lot of these Red Sox batters he was a disciple of the great hitting guru Walt Hriniak. He knew that a simple base hit was far more effective over the long-term than an occasional display of power. So Boggs shortened his swing and made good and consistent contact and earned himself the reputation as one of the best singles hitters in the history of the game—the American League version of Tony Gwynn, who had certainly worn me down a time or two.

The book on Boggs was that you couldn't strike him out. He had an innate feel for the strike zone, even as it shifted from umpire to umpire. And his swing was so precisely measured that he rarely missed. Was he dangerous, looming at the top of the Red Sox order? Not exactly—especially since he'd gone 0-7 against me in my first two series starts. But he wasn't the type of hitter I could expect to fool regularly, so he was a worry in the leadoff spot. With the bases empty, he couldn't hurt me; with runners on, he could knock me off the hill.

Next up was Marty Barrett, the Red Sox second baseman—the poster boy for what's known in baseball as "the pesky hitter." Marty was a grinder, a gamer. The book on him was to pitch him tight—to "jam the piss out of him," in the words of our pitching coach, Mel Stottlemyre. Marty had gotten a hit off of me in Game 1, and a double and single in Game 4, and every time I looked up, all series long, he seemed to be on base, so he was a worry, too.

Bill Buckner was in the three hole, and over in the National League we all knew him as one of the finest hitters of his generation. He was truly one of the great gentlemen of the game—and a tremendous athlete. He'd never gotten the ink of fellow first basemen, such as Keith Hernandez, probably because of his defense. But at the plate, this guy was right there, and after the way Game 6 ended, with Buckner kicking the play on a slow roller in the bottom of the tenth to allow the winning run to score, I didn't want to have to face him in a key spot. He had something to prove.

When you grow up watching the game, it imprints on your mind in a certain way. As a baseball-mad kid from Millbury, Massachusetts, I'd come of age as a young high school ballplayer just as Jim Rice burst on the scene with the home-town Sox—a team that made it all the way to the series, largely on the veteran-like contributions of Rice and his fellow rookie, center fielder Fred Lynn. Jim Rice was the first player I can remember who seemed to put the stadium on pause. He could dent the wall of the Green Monster with a simple flick of his massive wrists. Wherever you were, whatever you were doing, you had to stop and watch him hit. That's how it was in our house. I could be horsing around with my brothers, the game on in the background, and we'd hear Rice's name announced and we'd turn to face the television. Freddie Lynn might have won the Rookie of the Year and the MVP awards, and Carl Yastrzemski might have been putting an exclamation point to his Hall of Fame career, but Jim Rice was the man. And here he was, eleven years later, batting in the cleanup spot, still very much the man, still very much in my head, the one batter in the Red Sox lineup who could put the game on pause and hurt me in a big-time way. Or so I thought.

The right fielder, Dewey Evans, had one of the best arms in the game, a perennial Gold Glove outfielder, but a lot of people forget how potent he was at the plate. In some ways, his reputation was the opposite of Buckner's. His defense overshadowed his offense—but, let's be clear, this guy could hit! He was like a silent killer, looming behind Rice (and, sometimes, Baylor), but he was an easy guy to overlook in that lineup—in a pick-your-poison sort of way. Evans had taken Doc Gooden out in Game 2 at Shea, and he'd come up against me in Game 4 in a spot that could have put the game away before it really started. First inning, bases loaded, two out. Dewey hitting in the sixth spot, behind the designated hitter Baylor. I was struggling, early. There was Dewey at the plate, crouched low in his distinctive style, fouling off a couple of pitches, staring me down. Finally, I hung a mistake pitch he should have jumped on. Nine times out of ten, he would have crushed it, but he could only manage a weak grounder to Raffy Santana at short to end the inning.

That mistake pitch? As soon as it left my hand, I had that sick, sick feeling of wanting the ball back, but somehow Dewey just missed it and we were out of the inning. As I studied this Game 7 lineup that confrontation haunted me, because I knew he'd be waiting for me in the five spot, crouched low, hungry for another shot, waiting for me to make another mistake. Here again, he had something to prove.

My boyhood nemesis Rich Gedman was batting sixth. We had a long history. He went to St. Peter's High in Worcester; I went to St. John's in Shrewsbury—staunch rivals on the Central Massachusetts baseball circuit, going back a few generations. In those days, he mostly pitched and played first base. Me, I mostly played shortstop, but I was one of the better ballplayers on our team and I had a strong arm so I took my turn on the hill. I didn't really know what I was doing, but I had a decent fastball and good control—so in high school terms at least, I was ahead of the game. Gedman came to catching late in his career, but he could hit. More to the point, he could hit *me*. Hard. The only saving grace to our high school confrontations was that Richie didn't do a whole lot of damage—at least, not when we played at St. Peter's. Their home field, Lake Park, had some quirky outfield dimensions, with a too-short porch in right to accommodate a playground. The way it worked was that there was a line drawn in the fence, as you moved from the right-field foul pole (at just 250 feet) to right-center. A ball clearing the fence to the right of that line was a ground rule double; to the left, a home run. Richie could smoke it down the right-field line all day long, sometimes clearing the fence, the playground, and a couple of houses beyond that, and it would still just be a double, so I always pitched him so he could only pull the ball. He hit a lot of doubles off of me, that's for sure. He hit another off of me at Fenway in Game 4, a liner down the left-field line, and as he rounded first base I caught myself thinking, *Damn, Richie, enough already.*

(The silver lining here was that Mookie Wilson was able to throw Geddie out at second as he tried to will his single into a double, which would have put runners on second and third—and the takeaway for me on that mound was that I should have spent more time as a high school pitcher trying to get this guy to go the other way.)

The late Dave Henderson was like a wild card in that lineup. His sad, sudden passing at the age of 57, as this book was being copy-edited, leaves all of us who played alongside him to wonder yet again at the false sense of immortality we'd known as young athletes. The man played with such joy it's hard to think of him gone. He'd go on to have some big years in Oakland as my teammate, for a stretch. But the Sox had just picked him up from Seattle at the end of the 1986 season, and our book on him was paper-thin. Only thing I knew about Henderson was that he was built like a truck. I'd learned this the hard way: Game 1, seventh inning, one out. Jim Rice on second, Richie Gedman at the plate. Gedman hit a hard ground ball to second baseman Tim Teufel, and the ball just skidded through

Timmy's legs. He was in position to make a play, waiting on a hop that never came, allowing Rice to score what turned out to be the only run of the game. Mets fans remember the error because of the final score, but I remember the collision that came on the back of it. What happened was, as soon as the ball was hit, I moved instinctively toward first, which was what all Mets pitchers were taught to do in those days—the special circumstances of our right-side defense. Keith Hernandez played so far off the line at first, you never knew when a ball would end up in his glove—even a hard ground ball to the second baseman.

I was on my way to first when I saw the ball skip past Teufel, and in a split second I had one of those *Aw, crap!* moments where I realized I now had to break and spin toward home to back up a possible play at the plate. So I turned tail and went toward home at a full sprint, just as Dave Henderson went into his own full sprint from the on-deck circle on the third-base side of the field, to get into position to signal Rice to slide or not to slide (and, which side of the plate to reach for). Neither one of us saw the other guy, and we ran into each other head-on. I'm pretty sure it was the only home plate collision in World Series history involving the pitcher and the on-deck batter, away from the ball—a freak, fluke thing. Henderson was shaken up, but I think I got the worst of it, to where when I saw his name in the Game 7 lineup all I could think was how he'd knocked me flat.

Spike Owen sat in the eighth spot, and here all I could think was how much I loved watching this guy play. He was one of my favorite players, because of his *hum-baby!* attitude. Spike was always up, always chirping, always trying to make something happen. Throughout my time in the game, I'd look at guys in the opposing dugout and think, *I can play with him.* (Eventually, I did; on the long and winding roads of our dovetailing careers, we'd wind up teammates, too, for a brief stretch in Montreal.)

Baseball is like anything else—there are good guys and bad guys and every type in between, and Spike was one of the good guys; I loved his approach to the game, the way he was with his teammates. He was a switch hitter, but I never cared if a guy hit from both sides of the plate. To me, that's one of the most useless pieces of information you can share with a pitcher, because you only face him from one side of the plate. To me, Spike Owen was a left-handed hitter, and down at the bottom of the order I didn't think he'd give me much trouble. He had Bruce Hurst hitting behind him, of course, and *he* hadn't swung a bat in a professional game until this World Series, so whatever damage Spike could have done at the plate with a bona fide hitter batting behind him was softened by that empty spot in the order.

A side note on Spike Owen: I wasn't aware of it at the time, but I'd had a low moment with Spike's older brother Dave early on in my career. Oh, I knew full well that Dave Owen and I had had an unfortunate encounter, but I didn't know he and Spike were brothers, and I believe the connection rates a mention here. During my rookie year, I faced Rick Sutcliffe and the Cubs on a day when the wind was blowing out at Wrigley Field—never a good sign for a visiting pitcher. Sure enough, the game didn't go my way. I couldn't keep the ball in the park, and had just yielded two monster home runs in the fifth inning, to Keith Moreland and Ron Cey, giving up a 4–2 lead in the bargain. I was rattled. All of a sudden, the Cubs were up 7–4, and I was facing the light-hitting Dave Owen with the bases empty. He squared to bunt—and it set me off. There was no baseball reason for Dave Owen to bunt in this situation, and to this day I've got no idea if he was acting on his own or on the direction of his manager, Jim Frey. Either way, it felt to me like these Cubs wanted to embarrass me—like I hadn't already done a good job of *that* already.

So I drilled him, hard. I meant to hurt him, too. I was too green to know that this was just Dave Owen's game, getting on base in whatever ways he could, and the Cubs called me out on it. Both benches cleared and I got called every name in the book—deservedly so. It was a chickenshit move on my part. Davey Johnson left me in the game when the dustup settled, long enough to give up a single to Sutcliffe, which would have been a small indignity on top of a giant indignity if Rick hadn't been one of the best hitting pitchers in the game.

The indignity grew larger still when I was finally pulled off the field and had to walk back to the visitor's dugout beneath a storm of taunts and catcalls, as the Wrigley crowd let me know in no uncertain terms what a little shit I was for plunking one of their beloved Cubbies. That walk nearly set off a brawl, because one of the fans thought this was a good time to throw a cup of beer in my face, but cooler heads prevailed—an expression that seems particularly appropriate, now that I was wearing the contents of the cooler.

As a hitter, Spike was cut in a lot of the same ways as his brother—no pop, a guy who'd scratch and claw his way on base if you'd give him the chance. And with Bruce Hurst hitting behind him, I was determined not to give him the chance.

Hurst, for his part, was having a lights-out World Series. Like me, he was also making his third start, in his case after winning Game 1 and Game 5, allowing only two earned runs in seventeen innings. He was one of those dominant left-handers the Red Sox never seemed to know what to do with, like Bobby Ojeda and John Tudor—guys who went on to great careers in the National League after being traded away by a general manager who spent a little too much time stressing about the Green Monster. But for whatever reason, Bruce Hurst stayed in the fold, and he was dominating in this post-season. A strong outing in Game 7, and a Boston victory, would have surely earned him World Series MVP honors—although you could have said the same thing about me, behind a strong outing of my own and a Mets win.

What was curious here was that my thoughts ran to Bruce Hurst at all, in these pregame musings. If anything, I should have been thinking of him as a hitter, thinking how to pitch him if he came to the plate in a big spot. It always needles me when announcers and sportswriters make these big deals out of a marquee matchup between two top pitchers, because the reality is it's no matchup at all. It's a duel only in the most abstract sense, because of course the *showdown* happens between pitcher-and-batter, not pitcher-and-pitcher. It's more like a battle of the bands than a battle on the field—we take our turns on stage and do our thing, separately, in front of the same crowd. Typically, I didn't give the opposing pitcher a thought, any more than I considered whether or not I was facing a switch-hitter, but here I caught myself wondering what Hurstie might bring to the table, if my teammates would finally figure him out. And as I caught myself, I thought, *This can't be good, me agonizing over Hurst's stuff.*

I had my own stuff to worry about, after all.

RINSE AND REPEAT

Perhaps I should backtrack, just a little.

Yes, Monday dawned like a reboot. Yes, my family was still splayed all over my apartment, same as the day before. Yes, I was once again in my usual, growly pregame mood, same as the day before. Yes, those Red Sox hitters were lined up to face me, large and formidable, beaten and beatable, same as the day before. And yes, my arm felt great and I was good to go, same as the day before.

Yes, yes, yes . . .

I repeat myself, I know, but I repeat myself to show how on edge I was that second-time-around morning, because underneath these repeat motions there was something, well, different. Something I could not yet know.

In 1993, Harold Ramis came out with the movie *Groundhog Day,* and the first time I saw it I thought of this unsettling do-over in our schedule. If you've never seen it, Bill Murray plays a weatherman assigned to cover the famous Groundhog

Day ceremony in Punxsutawney, Pennsylvania, where he gets caught in a weird time loop and is forced to go through the same motions day after day after day. That's kind of like how things were for me, repeating my pregame rituals for the second day in a row—stuck, trying to get unstuck.

My heart was racing—just as it had been as I pulled up to Shea the day before. The stadium was hopping—just as it would have been if the weather had cooperated. It was Groundhog Day all over again. Oh, the crowd was louder, more energetic than I could have imagined, if I could have let myself imagine it, but as I stepped to the mound I tried to tune out the noise, to stay in my own head. Trouble was, there was noise enough in my own head. As I've written, I had one of those brains that kept working, whirring. If a thought found its way in, I could not let it go, so this was where that daylong rain delay started to do a number on me. With all that time to think and re-think my way through the Boston lineup, I talked myself into a hole. Worse: I talked myself into a hole and then threw a bunch of dirt on top of it. I was my own opponent, on a kind of knife-edge, which was absolutely *not* where I needed to be to start Game 7 of the World Series.

A game like this, you want to play like there's something on the line, like it all *means* something, but you don't want to carry too much pressure onto the field. Anyway, that's the idea. It's a tricky balance, tough to get it right. Game 1, it was all about getting our guys off to a good start, but there wasn't a whole lot of "do or die" to that home opener. Let's be clear, it was a statement game, we wanted to hold our home field advantage and put it out there that we were the team to beat, but it's not like we would have been up against it if we fell short. It would have sucked—and it did, as it turned out—but I gave myself an out in my thinking. I let myself relax, and free my mind of all those doomsday scenarios that might have found their way in. Same deal going into my Game 4 start in Boston; I found a way to let the positives from that first outing dictate my approach on this second pass. I told myself I had these guys figured out—and, at just that moment, in just those circumstances, I did.

Only now I wasn't doing such a great job dialing down those worries. The balance was off. My worries were like dirt, piling on, filling that big old hole. I worried the tables had turned and that after two starts, six or seven times through the order, these guys had *me* figured out. Game 1 and Game 4 should have been building blocks, but I worried that those efforts had been washed away by all that rain. I worried that all of that good work would now work against me. I worried that the extra day of rest had allowed the Red Sox to recharge, refresh, and maybe put the horror show of Game 6 behind them. I worried that we might have lost a step defensively, with Wally Backman and Lenny Dykstra now out of the lineup in the lefty-righty matchup dance that had Davey Johnson thinking their counterparts Tim Teufel and Mookie Wilson might give us a bit more of an edge against Bruce Hurst.

I worried. And then I worried some more. And then I worried that I was worrying.

Like a lot of ex-athletes, especially those who did their thing in the middle of the pack, the only games I really remember, the only games I agonize over, are the bad games, the false starts, the missteps and missed opportunities. I can semi-remember the good games, but they have become a blur over time. The details are lost to me. It's the bad games that have stayed with me, and this one is stuck to the bottom of my shoe—again, like I'd stepped in a steaming pile of shit.

What I remember most of all—the national anthem sung, the ceremonial first pitches tossed—was fretting over Wade Boggs in the leadoff spot. He had my attention, but not in the ways you might think. To repeat, Boggs was one of the best hitters of his time—of *all* time—and yet he wasn't exactly the sort of hitter to strike fear in an opposing pitcher. Too, there had been nothing in his recent résumé, nothing in his body of work this postseason to leave me reeling. I'd handled him well enough, easily enough in Game 1 and Game 4, but this just meant he'd had all that time to get a read on me. This just meant he was good and ready. It left me thinking I couldn't make a mistake, that I had to be precise and fine, which of course was no way to go after a batter—especially a batter with the pedigree of Wade Boggs. No, he couldn't hurt you with a single swing of the bat, not like Jim Rice or Don Baylor, but he could hurt you, make no mistake. Death by a thousand paper cuts, by seeing-eye singles . . . that's how a guy like Wade Boggs could hurt you.

And so he appeared in my vortex of worry, and as he stepped to the plate I told myself there was no way he was swinging at this first pitch. He didn't strike out a lot and was comfortable hitting with two strikes, so I felt sure he'd be taking. And he was, only I couldn't manage to get that first pitch over the plate. That was always a key marker for me, getting to that 0-1 count to start the game, but I missed big—high and wide. It didn't mean much, really, except now I told myself I had to be more precise, more fine. Told myself he'd be taking, still. Sitting on that first strike. So I came back with more of the same—this time, a little less high, a little less wide. This time, home plate umpire John Kibler threw up his right fist and signaled a called strike—a call that could have gone against me. *Should* have gone against me—I can see that now on the replay. It wasn't hard to tell, from sixty feet away, that Boggs wasn't happy with that call. He backed away, called time, ostensibly to wait for an overhead plane to pass so he could regain his focus, but I took the action to mean that he wanted to upset my rhythm in this early going, and put it out there to Kibler in this respectful way that he wasn't happy with the call.

It's a zero-sum game, this battle for focus between pitcher and batter. There's only so much of the stuff to go around. Whatever focus Boggs could claim for himself, it would come from me. Whatever I could grab, it would be at his expense, and in the tug-and-pull the confrontation would be won—or lost, depending.

We went back and forth in this way, and it got to me. It did. My focus became Boggs's focus; his distractions became mine. Understand, *getting to me* is a relative term. Every first batter, every game of my career, reaching all the way back to college and high school, there was a bagful of pregame jitters I carried with me to the mound. And here the bag was as heavy as it had ever been. I'd allowed the game to become bigger than me, bigger than usual—bigger, certainly, than it needed to be— and so even something as small as the batter stepping away from the plate to collect himself, to redouble his focus and cut mine in half, was enough to rankle.

For a moment—for *only* a moment—he was strengthened and I was diminished.

The plane passed and Boggs went back to work. So did I. Next pitch was right over the plate, right at the knees, but John Kibler gave this one to Boggs. I thought, *You've got to be shitting me.* That pitch was picture-perfect, just where I wanted it, and right away my thoughts started running, all the way to where I convinced myself Kibler wasn't going to give me a single call that night. I was diminished further still. Okay, so Kibler had just given me a gift on that 1-0 pitch, but now he'd taken it away, and in the exchange I decided he had it in for me. That's how tightly wound I was going in to this game. The littlest thing could get me going—and here I was, three pitches in, just about gone.

Still, I knew enough to set that one call aside, to not give away my disgust, my fear. The guys in the other dugout, they can smell all of that on you. They can. The umpire, he can smell it, too. Even the fans pick up on it. Make no mistake, it was an important pitch, at 1-1. You're moving deeper into the at bat, you want the count in your favor. The space between 1-2 and 2-1 is enormous, so that one pitch meant the world. It also meant that if Kibler wasn't going to give me that pitch at the knees, I was screwed. I needed that pitch, not just for this at bat, but for the entire game, for the series.

Even now, all these years later, that call just about knocks me on my ass.

In the interest of full disclosure, I should mention here that I'm leaning on old footage to lubricate my memory. There's no way I could pull the pitch-by-pitch, the play-by-play from these long-ago moments—not with any kind of accuracy. I know I just wrote that I carry my bad games with me, that I've played them through in my head on a kind of endless loop, but even these memories start to fade over time. At least, the specifics fall away and melt into one another, and at the other end I'm left with a general feeling of disappointment, an aching regret. And so I find myself reaching back across these decades with the eyes of a baseball analyst, which of course has been my job these past many years. And in many ways, it's a fresh take, because I haven't seen a frame of this footage since 1986. In fact, even then, I never watched tape on this game, so I'm taking it in from a whole new perspective. I am no longer a twenty-six-year-old big leaguer establishing myself, staring down these all-time greats on the biggest possible stage. No, I'm a fiftysomething former ballplayer, watching a younger, leaner, greener version of myself, bringing what I now know after a lifetime in the game to what I knew then after just a few seasons.

There were things I saw that night that I cannot see on the replay. There were things I remembered and carried with me for years that I can no longer recall. There were things that happened that never registered, the first time around. And there were things that didn't exactly happen in quite the same way I remembered them happening. Or maybe it's just that the camera angle was wrong, and whatever happened, whatever *actually* happened is forever lost to time and memory.

For one thing, the camera couldn't capture how Wade Boggs appeared to me just then. How imposing he'd seemed. It's not clear from the footage, but it takes me back just the same. I can remember how Boggs crowded the plate, how it struck me then, as if for the first time—me, thinking, *Man, oh man, this guy is all over me.* Another thing: he was a big, big man. Physically imposing. Most people, they look back on his career, they look at his numbers, they don't think of Wade Boggs in just this way, but he stood 6'2", maybe 200 pounds. You'd think a guy who hit .350 every year, all those looping line-drive singles, those doubles in the gap, would be a much smaller person. You think of a hitter in the scrappy, hustling mode, but that wasn't Boggs. No. And yet this is how I remember him when I faced him. In my mind, he was a scrappy, hustling .350 hitter waiting me out.

Also, I'm remembering the crowd as I look back. I'm remembering the noise, the exuberance, but I'm remembering it in an intellectual way. I'm framing the moment, but when I was in its middle, out there on that mound, I was in a kind of bubble. There was no crowd. There was no noise. There was just me, just Boggs, just Gary Carter behind the plate, just home plate umpire John Kibler behind him. Just the four of us. And here's the thing: going in, John Kibler wasn't even a thought in my mind, but now he was in the mix. Now I had to worry about his strike zone, him not giving me that call at the knees, him getting in the way of what I had to do.

I was all about my fastball, those first few pitches. This wasn't a game plan, a strategy, it's just how it was, so I came back with another fastball, pretty much in the same spot, and Boggs fouled it off. I knew I couldn't fool this guy, so I tried to blow it past him. Kid didn't agree with me, behind the plate. I had to shake him off three or four times back at 1-1, but I was determined to lean on my heater, to save the rest of my stuff for later, to show the best pure hitter in the game that he couldn't touch me. I was arrogant, but I told myself I'd earned the right to be arrogant. I'd shut these guys down twice already.

It was a hittable pitch, but Boggs just missed it, and it pissed him off that he'd just missed it. I was pissed, too, that I'd given him something to hit. But he seemed to have a better handle on his frustration. And if he wasn't the one who was more composed, he wasn't letting on. He stepped back in, close, looking for his pitch. I could either jam him or come in low and go at him again. So what did I do? I went low and away—another fastball, this one even farther outside than the first pitch of the game.

Now the count was full, and this gave me pause. I never wanted to get into one of those long, drawn-out battles with the first batter of the game,. The idea was to dispatch the lead-off man and get on with it, but Boggs was the kind of patient, painstaking hitter who could foul off pitch after pitch, waiting for me to make a mistake. If I let him do that, it would set a down tone for the rest of the game, even if I'd managed to get him out. Still, at 3-2, I couldn't afford to be too precise, or too fine, and I couldn't count on Boggs chasing a pitch outside the strike zone, so it felt to me like I had no choice but to blow one by him. I went at him with yet another fastball, a shade low and away.

Boggs was on it. He sliced a hard line drive toward short—a bullet that just happened to find the glove of our shortstop Rafael Santana, who only had to move a half step to make the grab, chest high. Boggs had waited me out, waited on his pitch, got inside my head, and as Raffy whipped the ball around to Teufel at second and then on to Keith Hernandez at first, I watched as Boggs returned dejectedly to the Red Sox dugout and I counted myself lucky. I thought, *Man, that could have been trouble.*

Next up was Marty Barrett—and here, looking at tape, I can't help but think, *This is what scrappy looks like.* He cut a completely different figure at the plate from Boggs—same result, over the past week or so, but you'd never know it to look at him. Already, Barrett had had a handful of broken-bat hits this series, so things were falling his way. Baseball can be funny that way. You can count on a hitter to hit to the back of his baseball card over time—meaning his career stat lines are a reliable predictor of future outcomes—but over a short stretch, a Mario Mendoza can hit like Ty Cobb. In a seven-game series, the only reliable predictors are that your opponents are professional hitters, capable of anything. Barrett came into the game hitting .480 over the first six games. Like Boggs, he crowded the plate. Like Boggs, he wanted to make me work. He wanted the ball middle of the plate, away, so I wasted one inside and low—close enough he had to kind of skip out of the way of it. Not exactly a brushback pitch, but it would give me back some of the plate.

Jam the piss out of him.

I could hear Mel Stottlemyre's voice in my head, so I came back inside on the second pitch, also low, but this one caught the corner for a called strike. In a lot of ways, it was the same sequence, the same approach I'd just taken with Boggs. You miss big on the first pitch and then you dial it back, miss a little less big, maybe catch a call.

At 1-1, I moved the ball back across the plate even farther—another fastball, this one right over at the knees for a called strike two. Not exactly where Barrett seemed to want it, but with each pitch I was baiting him, inching toward his sweet spot, hoping to get him to offer at it. Finally, at 1-2, he did—at another fastball at the knees. He lofted a soft fly ball to Darryl Strawberry in shallow right field, but at the crack of the bat I caught myself thinking, *Is this another Marty Barrett hit*? That's how hot Barrett had been, but also how tentative I was during these early moments. When I was on my game and feeling it, a soft, nothing liner like this one, I'd hear that same crack of the bat and know I'd won the battle. But these were the kinds of hits that had been dropping for Barrett, and when you're on a roll like he was on a roll—he'd hit safely in all six games, thus far—you stand across from him and think the whole world is going his way.

Happily, this one had enough loft to it to allow Darryl to run underneath to make the grab, and I'd bought myself two quick outs with no damage to show for it other than a glaring lack of confidence—which, hopefully, nobody recognized but me.

Bill Buckner followed Barrett in the lineup, and even before his name was announced Mets fans started giving it to him—a semi-derisive standing ovation, loud enough to pierce whatever firewalls I'd put up in my head to block out the crowd noise. I took it in, understood it for what it was, but at the same time I tried not to pay attention to it. I tuned it out, waited it out. That Buckner error in Game 6 meant nothing to me just then. It could have happened to anyone—ball took a bad bounce (a bad *no* bounce), that's all. I had such enormous respect for Bill Buckner, as did anyone who'd ever played alongside him or against him, that I couldn't help but feel for him in that moment. And he was such a tough competitor I had to think he'd find a way to use whatever emotions had attached to Saturday night's extra-inning miscue to somehow redeem himself, so I was relieved to see him here with the bases empty.

Looking back, I've wondered about that standing ovation. It wasn't a full-on, full-throated, full-stadium jeer; it was one of those isolated deals. There were whole sections of fans on their feet, mock-cheering, holding their handmade Buckner banners high, and then there were pockets of fans every here and there doing more of the same, but I don't think it was a mean-spirited display. There was no taunting or baiting, as there seemed to be whenever the crowd aimed its signature singsong chant at our syllabically correct foes.

(Just now, for Marty Barrett: *M-a-a-a-r-t-e-e-e! M-a-a-a-r-t-e-e-e!*)

No, with Buckner, it felt to me like the ovation was a true show of appreciation—better, a true show of *gratitude*. Without Buckner, these diehards were saying, we wouldn't be here. Without Buckner, this glorious season would have come to an inglorious end. Without Buckner, our Metsies would not have lived to fight another day. To Red Sox fans, Buckner might have been the goat, but to Mets fans he was a conquering hero, and so they gave thanks, in what ways they could. And underneath those thanks, in some way, was the message that these thinking, feeling fans understood that Buckner had caught a bad break, that he could not be defined by that one defining miscue.

Buckner had that classic Walt Hriniak–type stance,

crouched low on the left side of the plate, the bat just about resting on his left shoulder, his chin nearly kissing his right shoulder, his weight on his back foot. I started him out with another fastball, low and away. John Kibler said with his fist that it caught the corner, and I was inclined to agree with him, but Buckner seemed to want to argue the point. He actually spun around to face the umpire, stare him down a bit, let him know what he thought of the call, but I couldn't tell if he actually said anything. Buckner flashed Kibler a look, was all, and sometimes, when you're a veteran player, a look is all you need—not unlike the way Boggs had stepped out after the second pitch of the game, the fastball high and outside that was called a strike, letting it be known that Kibler owed him one.

Here again, the call could have gone either way—and there was a time early on in my career when it would have gone against me. As a rookie, on into my second full season, there was so much sink on my fastball I ended up walking a lot of hitters. But over time, as I'd cycled through the National League umpire corps, I developed a bit of a reputation, and on the back of that reputation I started getting that call. It's like they had a meeting, all these umpires, and collectively decided, *Hey, this kid Darling looks like he's gonna be a decent pitcher. Looks like he'll be around for a while.* And now, three full years into my career, this first pitch to Buckner was the result.

Strike one.

The crowd, a little less well-meaning now, a little less grateful and welcoming, noticed Buckner's reaction to the call and started in on him all over again:

Bill-eee! Bill-eee!

I don't think I picked up on this at the time, but it was clear on the replay, and I have to think it registered in some way while I was out there on the mound. What I do recall firsthand is thinking that I had Buckner guessing, so I followed with my first breaking ball of the night. I'd thrown eleven straight fastballs to this point, most of them tailing away, and it seemed like a good time to switch things up. Again, this wasn't our game plan going in, and it had as much to do with Kid and Mel as it did with me. With Kid, he knew I was pumped, knew I needed to stay pumped for these first few batters, so he was content to let me air it out—other than those few times he wasn't. With Mel, he didn't like to micromanage his pitchers once the game was under way. He left it to his catcher to talk strategy, approach—other than those few times he'd find me in the dugout between innings to go over a couple of things.

Buckner was waiting on the curve and put a good swing on it, lashed a hard grounder down the first-base line—again, just foul. I thought, *Okay, so much for my breaking ball.* At 0-2, I came back with another tailing fastball, which was turning into my trademark pitch in this opening frame, but here it set me up for what would come next. Watching the replay, I like what I was trying to do here with Buckner. I like the sequence: first pitch, fastball, I get the call; second pitch, curve ball down, he fouls it off; third pitch, another fastball, away. I'd set it up so I had to come inside with the next pitch. Only, Buckner certainly knew I had to come inside with the next pitch. And *I* knew that he knew, and *he* knew that I knew that he knew, and on and on—no surprises here.

Trouble was I didn't put the ball quite where I wanted it.

I came in low, on the inside half of the plate, and Buckner sliced a lazy fly ball down the left-field line, just foul. For a beat or two, it looked like it might drop, and Buckner was halfway to second when it came down, so here again it felt to me like I'd gotten away with something. And Buckner, as he zagged across the diamond on the first-base side of the mound, looked like he'd hurt himself rounding the bag. He was walking gingerly and, sure enough, you could see on the replay he'd kind of stumbled as he made the turn toward second.

No big thing—something to notice, but no big thing.

Here I should have followed with another pitch inside, but I came back with an off-speed pitch outside, just to mix things up, and then at 2-2 Buckner lunged at a fastball off the plate and tapped a bouncer between first and second for a single—a good pitch, but I didn't get away with it.

It was a great at bat for Buckner, especially coming off the ignominy of Saturday night. Think about that: his first at bat after what was one of the most disastrous defensive plays in the history of the World Series, and it cost his team the game and for the moment the series, and he comes back and gets a hit. It's a tribute to the kind of player he was—the kind of *competitor* he was. But it also showed how the game is played when everyone is on this same knife-edge. Nine times out of ten, that same ground ball, off this same hitter, in this same spot, Keith Hernandez would have fielded it easily, but here it was just beyond his reach. Why? Because he'd thought Gary Carter had called for the splitter, assumed the ball would be pulled, so he was leaning left when the ball was hit and by the time he went right it was just out of reach.

A read like that could have meant the difference between a one-two-three inning and a two-out rally.

Two out. One on. Jim Rice at the plate.

What this meant, in purely mechanical terms, was that it turned me around and forced me to pitch from the stretch. First time that happens in a game is always interesting. You prepare for it. You pitch from the stretch in the bullpen, but then you go out and find your rhythm and it's as if you've shut one valve and switched on another. Here I'd thrown sixteen pitches, and my fastball was working, and I had a nice fluidity going, and all of a sudden I had to hold the runner on. Granted, that runner was Bill Buckner, on a bum set of wheels. There was no way he was running, but I had to keep him close, honest. So now I had a whole new worry to add to the bagful I'd toted out to the mound with me to start the game—I worried I'd lose my mojo.

Now, it's not like I'd come out all gangbusters. It's not like I was blowing these Red Sox hitters away. Not even close. I hadn't really settled into the game just yet, hadn't pitched with any real confidence, but my fastball was working in such a way that it was something to build on. When you've got your fastball, it's a little like having the wind at your back. The game flows just a little more easily. The opposing hitters, it's like they're moving into the wind. So there was that.

Also, there's pitching from the stretch and there's *pitching from the stretch*. (Emphasis added.) Usually when you're in the stretch, you're thinking about the base runner as well as the hitter, but like I said, this wasn't an issue. Here I wasn't really paying attention to Buckner because I knew he couldn't hurt me. *Jim Rice* . . . he could hurt me, so he's the one who had my full attention.

Rice was out in front of the first pitch—a fastball down the middle—so right away I had him 0-1. But then I came back and threw a pitch in the dirt, which Kid managed to keep in front of him. At 1-1, I busted Rice inside with a fastball, on the fists, and he could only foul it back to put the count at 1-2. He was in the habit back then of choking up on the bat—something he did off and on for most of his career, but here it was more pronounced so I aimed for the handle.

He fouled off another pitch before I hung one right over the plate, maybe a little low, and he went the other way with it, hard. Darryl Strawberry broke to his left on the swing, got a good jump. Always, with Strawberry, he had this kind of easy, loping gait, made it seem like he wasn't really running as fast as he could—but, man, he could fly! He had those long, long legs, those deep, graceful strides, and he covered a lot of territory without a whole lot of apparent effort. So there he was, loping gracefully toward the right-field foul pole, his right arm extended, chasing down this pea off the bat of Jim Rice, and it felt to me like the ball would fall for a double, at least. But Strawberry just kept running, never a doubt in his mind that he'd get to where the ball was going a beat ahead of the ball. Sure enough, he ran right through the ball and backhanded it like he was shagging flies, and just like that we were out of the inning.

Wasn't exactly a clean sheet, but it did the job, and I walked purposefully, confidently back to the dugout, thinking, *Okay, boys, let's get it done.*

STRUTTING OUR STUFF

This *let's get it done* mantra was like a theme to our season. Say what you will about the character and chemistry of that 1986 Mets team, there was a haughtiness that attached itself to us, a bluster, and here in the last game of the season, the finish line in sight, it could only bubble forth. If you were a Mets fan back then, if you lived in New York, if you followed baseball even in a sidelong way, you'll know that we moved about the city like we owned the place. Oh, man, there was some serious swagger to our game, to the ways we carried ourselves off the field. It's like we felt we were *entitled* to win, like we somehow deserved it. We were cocky as hell—you could see it in our approach. You could see it in the way Mel Stottlemyre sent me home at the end of the eighth inning of Game 6, after we'd tied the game at 3–3. We were so confident, so arrogant, so dead solid certain that we were bound to be world champions, we put the notches on our belts before we earned them.

We were a team of destiny, we all believed, and a part of that destiny was to go down in the record books as one of the greatest teams of all time. To a man, we would have said it was a given. Winning was our birthright, our responsibility. Nothing less would do, and moving about as if nothing less would do fairly defined our demeanor. Forget that we'd yet to win *anything,* really, other than a bunch of regular season games. That didn't matter. This World Series was *ours*—ours to lose, anyway. (And we very nearly did just that, a couple of times over.)

Of course, the way things played out, we found a way to turn one of the greatest teams of all time into a team that simply had a great year—but hey, you've got to play the games before you write the history. You've got to earn your stripes before you wear them—only, we were too young, too full of ourselves to realize this just then, but it became clear to each of us, in turn, in time. It was the time of our lives, our season in the sun, our moment to shine, shine, shine.

Looking back, of course, we didn't take such good care of the great gifts we'd been given—I believe that's a fair assessment. We took our blessings for granted; we danced to our own damn tune.

Much has been written and whispered about the wild escapades of our merry band of brothers that year. Some of that has been in the form of speculation, and before I return to the action on the field it's probably a good idea to separate the facts from the fictions in this regard—or, at least, what I *know* to be the facts. Foremost among these are the stories of drug use that seemed to follow us around like that bowl of oatmeal in those old Maypo commercials—cocaine, mostly. Now, a few of my teammates have spoken bravely about their strug-gles with cocaine, but I'm not about to throw them back under the team bus here. I can only write what I know, what I've seen, and when it came to cocaine I didn't have a clue. That's for my teammates to discuss, on their own terms—or not. Me, I can only write about my own experiences and observations, and I think it's also fair to say that I was a bit of a wet blanket when it came to recreational drug use. Even at Yale, I was com-pletely clueless regarding the extracurricular antics of some of my classmates. Sure, I'd been to parties where the coke was flowing freely—that was just how things were on college cam-puses in the early 1980s, how they were in New York City in the middle 1980s. That was the scene. But these weren't *team* parties, and I can honestly say that I never once saw one of my teammates snort, shoot, smoke, or otherwise ingest cocaine—hand on the Bible.

That said, I knew full well this type of thing was going on and, for the most part, I knew who was doing what. It was understood in and around the Mets clubhouse, even though it wasn't talked about, except maybe in hushed tones. We had our share of shady characters skulking around. Guys were making frequent trips to the bathroom on team flights, and it was generally assumed that they were doing blow; on road trips, guys were ducking out of the clubhouse early, heading to some wild party or other. There were knowing glances darting back and forth—but what the hell did I know, really? I'd heard from my cop friends on Long Island—in Port Washing-ton, where a lot of guys lived—that they were being called to this or that player's home to follow up on a tip or a complaint, but here, too, I wasn't about to jump to any conclusions based on rumors or hearsay. I knew what I needed to know—as much as I *wanted* to know, let's just say that.

Truth was I had no idea what it was like to do blow. Naively, I figured it was just like smoking pot or drinking a few too many beers. But then I'd hear stories of some of my teammates spiraling out of control, setting off on these reckless tears, and it didn't take a genius to know they'd taken things to a whole other level.

Weed was a little more prevalent—a little more out in the open, at least. But even here, guys were secretive about their habits. I knew from personal observation that there were a bunch of guys on the team who smoked regularly, but I'm not about to give them up here; again, that's for them to do, if they so choose. About the only vices that were openly pursued were alcohol and amphetamines. When I first came up, there was a jar of pills that was kept in a prominent place—prominent, that is, if you knew where to look for it. It was called the jar because, come on, baseball players weren't the most creative bunch. It became a part of our language, our shorthand. If someone was scrambling, trying to mask an ache or a pain, or maybe to recover from an injury, he'd say, "I'm in the jar today."

Each pill had its own name. The five-milligram amphetamines were known as white crosses—and these were passed around like candy, if that was your bag. The heavier doses were black beauties. Remember, this was well before the common use of steroids and other performance-enhancing drugs; in many ways, you could make the argument that the drugs of choice in our clubhouse were more performance *reducing* than anything else. But most starting pitchers were loath to mess with any chemicals that might mess with their mind-set—anyway, *I* was. You've got all that time between starts, the last thing you want is to be anxious and on edge for four days; if anything, you want something to take the edge *off*.

Still, the jar was very much in evidence, very much a part of our team "chemistry," even though the jar itself had disappeared by the 1986 season. We continued to use the same language, though, so you could still hear the terminology on the team plane and in the clubhouse, but the pill-taking became much more secretive. You either understood the euphemism—or you didn't, because it didn't apply. It was no longer out in the open. The talk went underground, but even there you'd continue to hear comments like, "Hey, I did a couple of white crosses but that didn't do it so I threw a black beauty on top and it was perfect." You'd see guys toward the end of a game, maybe getting ready for their final at bat, double-back into the locker room to chug a beer to "re-kick the bean" so they could step to the plate completely wired and focused and dialed in. They had it down to a science, with precision timing. They'd do that thing where you poke a hole in the can so the beer would flow shotgun-style. They'd time it so that they were due to hit third or fourth that inning, and in their minds that rush of beer would kind of jump-start the amphetamines and get back to how they were feeling early on in the game—pumped, jacked, good to go. How they came up with this recipe, this ritual, I'll never know, but it seemed to do the trick; they'd get this rush of confidence that was through the roof and step to the plate like the world-beaters they were born to be.

Understand, there was no party in the use of these drugs—that part happened off the field, away from the game.

No, this was all business. This was the care and feeding of the professional athlete. The "jar" was like our traveling medicine cabinet, a way to chase the aches and pains. You'd walk into the clubhouse and catch one of your teammates sitting in front of his locker looking like he'd just been through a spin cycle. There'd be dark circles under his eyes. The simplest movements would be accompanied by the groans of an old, beaten-down man. It would be the middle of August—game 141 on the schedule, say—the dog days of the dog days, and this poor guy could barely stand and straighten his knees because of all the abrasions running up and down his legs. He'd be bruised from head to toe, from being plunked by a season's worth of pitches. He'd have a couple of broken bones in his hands, but he was determined to play through his injuries, to see his way to the butt end of the schedule. Maybe he was playing for his next contract, scrambling to keep his job over some upstart rookie.

These pick-me-up type drugs were just a way to mask or chase the pain. They were part of the landscape; they'd been around the game for generations. In the era of Mays and Aaron, the heroes of my growing up, it was all about red juice or Cuban coffee—the brews found in virtually every clubhouse, spiked with amphetamines and whatever else the prevailing "wisdom" suggested. Guys would down a cup, grab a bat, and head out for the most fearsome batting practice session you'd ever seen.

This was how you played 155 games a season, because even your horses needed a day off every here and there. This was how you got paid, how you cheated time. You found a way to power through, and for a great many of us this could only happen with a pharmaceutical assist. The perception back then was that you couldn't possibly make it to the end of the season without some carefully timed fistfuls of pills, and a shotgun blast of beer to wash them all down. You couldn't get there on your own. But, of course, you could. Absolutely you could. It's just that most of us didn't trust that you could.

The white crosses and black beauties and all the colors and varieties in between were such a big part of our approach to the game, we still talk about it. The guys I played with, we get together and reminisce. We marvel, really, at the shit some of our teammates put into their bodies . . . into *our* bodies. We run the numbers in our head, try to calculate how many milligrams of amphetamines were actually in play during that great World Series run. Go around the diamond; do the math. Ten milligrams here, twenty there, maybe thirty over there . . . up and down the lineup, all across the field, we were shot through with so much of the stuff it's hard to imagine how we thought it could shake out to the good.

The reality was, with that many guys, popping that many pills, you could begin to guess how things would go. There were predictable outcomes. There'd be a *failure to launch*— meaning, you'd lay in just the right cocktail of pills, and time it just right, and still the body would fail to respond. You'd see guys walking around the clubhouse with this panicked look in their eyes, because they'd done everything they could to get up and ready for the game, never counting on the fact that the physiology of the human body can change from day to day. Or there'd be an ill-timed *prelaunch*—meaning, guys would be firing on all cylinders before the game even started, setting the world on fire in BP, bouncing off the clubhouse walls like a pinball, only to crash and burn by the first inning. And then there'd be the *perfect storm*—meaning, you'd find yourself in that sweet spot where anything was possible, where you get your four hits on a day game after a night game, where nothing can touch you. Maybe you drove to the stadium wondering how the hell you'd lift your arm over your head, and you end up playing the game of your life.

Basically, you'd never know how things would go. All you could do was reach for the jar and hope for the best—and when the best wasn't happening, you'd reach for a glass of milk. That was a line you'd hear all the time—"Go have a glass of milk!"—because the milk would coat your stomach and mitigate some of the effects of the amphetamines, keep you from peaking too early. Or, something. It took me awhile to figure out why all these guys were downing all these glasses of milk in such a big hurry, but then, if you weren't "in the jar," some of the language and some of the routines were elusive.

Still, you figured it out soon enough. Everyone was just doing what they thought they needed to do to survive.

The party happened away from the field, away from the clubhouse, and what I remember best about the spirit of that 1986 Mets team was our sense of abandon. Sure, there was a whole lot of *reckless* abandon to our behavior, but let's look past that *reckless* qualifier and focus on the pure shot of joy that coursed through our team that season. It was everywhere and all around. Think of it: to be young and on top of your game, the city of all cities at your feet, a world of possibilities within reach. . . . we were invulnerable, untouchable. The mood of the clubhouse, all season long, was fairly euphoric—each moment thick with the weight of great expectations and unlimited possibilities.

Anyway, there was no shortage of things to celebrate, and our celebrations were almost always set to music. I was the un-official deejay on team trips. I had one of those big old boom boxes. (Remember those suckers?) The boom box was the size of a small valise, powered by ten D batteries. I used to carry an extra set of ten batteries to make sure the thing kept firing on those long East Coast/West Coast flights. I also traveled with a couple hundred CDs and worried constantly over my play-list. (CDs—remember *those* suckers?) I tried to thematically honor the mood, the moment. After a tough loss, I'd play a lot of slow, mournful ballads. On the bus back to the hotel, I'd keep it low, chill. And then, on the plane, I'd crank up the volume and blast some really raucous tunes—power pop, metal, classic rock, whatever I thought fit the mood.

My thing was to sit at the back of the plane, the very last row on the left side as you walked down the aisle. Guys would cluster by my seat, looking to get their songs on my air:

Hey, R.J., play this.

Hey, R.J., play that.

In those days, the coaches, the front office staff, even the beat writers all sat up in first class, so we were way, way re-moved from the brass. One by one, they'd all come back to check out our scene: Tim McCarver, Ralph Kiner, Joe Durso from the *Times,* Marty Noble from *Newsday.* Davey Johnson would usually make an appearance, but only after we got the heat going in the cabin, only after the party was up and started. He'd pretend to dance down the aisle as he approached, like the hardly cool dad crashing his kids' basement bash—but, really, he was a lot of fun. If he had something to say, something about the game, or maybe one of us needed a talking-to following some piece of off-field shenanigans, he'd find a way to get his point across. It wasn't always the *best* way, as I will soon share, but the message was always delivered. Once, after he'd kept Darryl Strawberry out of the lineup because our star right fielder was under the weather, Davey turned after his back-of-the-plane visit and said, "Keep it down, Ronnie. Don't want to keep Darryl from getting his rest."

More than a little sarcastic, letting us know he thought Darryl's "day off" was bullshit.

And Straw, he could read between the lines as well as anyone. He said, "Fuck you, Davey."

That's just how we were wired—we were always talking shit—and Davey Johnson helped to set that loose tone. Other managers would have been pissed. They wouldn't tolerate that kind of back talk, even from a star player. But to Davey it was all in good fun, and we came to appreciate that it was all in good fun.

Davey and I had a bit of a contentious relationship. There were a lot of father-son aspects to it, but there was an ongoing tension. Anyway, I already had a father—a man I loved without reservation. I loved Davey, too, but with reservations. He was tough on me. As a former position player, he didn't have the softest place in his heart for us pitchers. You see that a lot around baseball lifers like Davey. When you're out there every day, making things happen, there's a tendency to think of the pitchers on your team as somehow *less than*. It's the story of the game. And for a guy like Davey Johnson, who played on those great Baltimore Orioles teams of the 1960s and '70s, it must have felt like he was toiling in the shadows of that dominant pitching staff: Jim Palmer, Mike Cuellar, Pat Dobson, Dave McNally . . . twenty-game winners all for the 1971 Baltimore team that lost to Pittsburgh in the World Series.

If you remember, Baltimore manager Earl Weaver had his own contentious relationship going with Jim Palmer, who would go on to become one of the premier pitchers of his generation, but in the Orioles clubhouse he was also Weaver's whipping boy. Earl Weaver beat up on Jim Palmer in the press, in the dugout, in the clubhouse, away from view—not physically, of course, but verbally. Things never got quite that bad between me and Davey, he never treated me shabbily, but I was the one guy on our staff he would single out and criticize in a public way. I understand this now, see that this was part of Davey's style—his people skills on piss-poor display—but at the time it just set me off. See, Davey had come of age as a ballplayer watching his manager light a fire under his team by riding one of his most prominent pitchers. He was one of those guys who'd been taught to think it was nothing for a pitcher to throw strikes. *How can you miss with the 0-2 pitch? How can you walk that guy on four pitches?* Like a lot of everyday players, he had no idea what it was like for a pitcher out there on that mound. This was how he'd been conditioned, and here I was, in his sights. He couldn't go after Sid Fernandez, because Sid was too fragile—he had that loose, laid-back persona he'd brought with him from Hawaii, which could never have fit alongside the ball-busting Davey seemed inclined to administer. He couldn't go after Bobby Ojeda, because Bobby had just joined our team and Davey didn't really know him all that well. Last thing he would have wanted was to mess with

Bobby O's head in such a way that he went off the rails. And he couldn't go after Dwight Gooden, because Doc was Davey's meal ticket, our name-above-the-title rock star, the face of the franchise. Me, I was the kid from Yale with halfway decent stuff who could probably take whatever Davey was dishing out—like Darryl in the back of the plane telling him to fuck off, I could give as good as I got.

So he dished, usually in a once-removed way, to reporters or teammates. His style was to make sure his comments got back to me, but he rarely put them to me directly. It was like a clubhouse version of telephone, that little-kid game we all used to play, where you whisper something into someone's ear, and he whispers it into the next kid's ear, and so on down the line. Davey would put one of his criticisms out into the world and wait for it to find me. In a conversation about me and Doc, for example, he'd say something like, "How can Dwight be so good at nineteen years old, and Darling's twenty-two and still learning?"

There might have been some truth to what he was saying, even though it rankled to hear him say it in this once-removed way. In this example, it was certainly true that I hadn't really *pitched* until college, so of course I was still learning, but Davey could have spoken to me directly. I didn't have Doc's repertoire of pitches. I didn't have his velocity, his curve, his raw talent, and yet, somehow, I found a way to win ball games and make a place for myself on that staff.

These days, it's become fashionable to compare a dominant, top-to-bottom pitching staff with those great Orioles starters from 1971, but the 1986 Mets pitchers were probably the first to rate the comparison. In fact, *Sports Illustrated* did a cover story on us in its August 25, 1986, issue, in the fat middle of our season. Somehow, I wound up on the cover, beneath the headline, "Armed Force: Ron Darling of the Pitching-Rich Mets."

We played to those expectations all season long, but in Davey's mind at least, I was the low-hanging fruit of our pitching corps, so he kept picking at me. Once, I'd had a decent-enough start at Philadelphia. I didn't have my best stuff that day, giving up five earned runs in just five innings of work. I threw a lot of pitches, and Davey went after me in the papers following the game. He told reporters that if I didn't start using my breaking ball I'd never become the pitcher I was meant to be—some nonsense like that. I hated that I had to hear this type of thing in the press. If Davey had come to me directly, I probably would have responded to him, because I was always pretty good about listening to constructive criticism from my coaches, but here I went another way. In my next start, I went out and threw a five-hit shutout against the Pirates at Shea. I struck out 11 Pittsburgh hitters, and I made it a special point not to throw a single breaking ball—a little "fuck you" to my manager.

With Doc, Davey would probably have looked at my middling performance in the first game and said something like, "This guy's such a gamer. Even when he doesn't have his best stuff, he finds a way to win." With me, it was all about how much I still had to learn—and I did, only here the lesson had mostly to do with how to set aside your manager's own insecurities and personality flaws in such a way that you could still find a way to work together toward a common goal.

Back to the plane. Back to the wild rumpus. We were all in on the same ride, all of us together, and it didn't much matter if you were the manager or the last guy on the bench . . . we were at the same party, after all.

It wasn't enough just to crank those tunes on the team plane. It wasn't enough to dance our weary asses off. We had to sing, too—top of our lungs–type singing—and it fell to me to cherry-pick from my collection to find songs we all knew, tunes we could all carry. "Suzie Q" by Creedence Clearwater Revival was one of our greatest hits; it never failed to get the cabin going. There'd be flight attendants sitting in our laps, perched on our armrests, belting it out right along with us, drinking in the same good time.

We flew mostly charters in those days. Once or twice a season, we'd fly those big commercial jets with the upstairs piano lounge. The team would book the first-class cabin, and we'd have at it. But mostly it was just us, flying those friendly skies as if we owned them—and we did.

Sometimes, our antics made headlines. This was regrettable, but on one night in particular, it was also inevitable. Turned out I was at the center of it all—a low moment on a string of high notes. We were in Houston, doing our thing at a place called Cooter's. We were having a rowdy, rollicking good time, nothing out of the ordinary, when our second baseman Tim Teufel joined us, mid-rollick. Until Timmy arrived, there was no good reason for us to be having a good time; we'd just lost to the Astros 3–0, and yours truly was the losing pitcher. But Timmy's wife had just had a baby, he'd been away from the team for a couple of days, and he was fresh off the plane and ready to rejoin our traveling circus. He'd probably been up for two days straight, shuttling to his wife in the delivery room and then back to us, and best I could tell he'd had a couple of pops on the flight to Houston, so he was in a mood to celebrate. And we were in the mood to help him out.

That's what teammates are for, right?

I can't say for sure how long we celebrated, or even how hard we celebrated, but last call came around soon enough— and our thing was, whenever we heard "last call," we looked to make a quick exit. That was the drill because the last thing we needed was for the lights to go on and the place start to thin, and all of a sudden we'd be calling all this extra attention to ourselves. We started for the door. All of us, that is, except for Timmy, who was determined to down the last of his beer—a Heineken, as the news accounts would later note.

He said, "Listen, Ronnie. I'm just gonna finish my beer. I'll hide it in my coat. I just had a baby. I'll drink it in the cab back to the hotel."

I thought, *No big thing*.

Except it was. Didn't have to be, but it was. You see, in Houston, like in a lot of cities, local club owners tended to hire off-duty policemen to work security, and these guys tended to be by the book. Worse, they went about their moonlighting like they had something to prove. A typical bouncer, you could sometimes get him to look the other way, but an off-duty cop . . . well, not so much, and here it worked out that one of these off-duty guys flagged Timmy down as he was looking to leave with his beer. Oh, and one more thing: it also worked out, the way it always does, that the local cops tended to root, root, root for their home teams, so we weren't about to get any special treatment. In fact, we could pretty much count on these guys to give us a hard time, deserving or no.

Sure enough, that's just what happened. We were standing

outside, by these two giant flower boxes that framed the Cooter's entryway, when one of the cops started hassling Timmy about this one rogue beer. Timmy was harmless, but insistent; he was a new dad; there was everything to celebrate; life was good; he was going to finish his Heineken, thank you very much. This one security cop, he was just as insistent; he wasn't about to be disrespected; life maybe wasn't so good that he had to tolerate even the benign misbehavior of these visiting athletes; the rules were meant to be followed and he was meant to enforce them and we were meant to be caught in the cross fire. Timmy and this one cop went back and forth on this for a bit. Soon, another cop joined in, and the hassling turned ugly. Timmy, for his part, wasn't budging. He had some bluster to him, like the rest of us, and he was deep into celebratory mode, so he didn't see this show of off-duty force for what it was—not at first, and by the time he did it was too late.

By that point, I'd heard one of the security cops say, "Break his arm, he's with the Mets."

It might have just been something to say, a whispered aside between buddies on the fake force, but then he repeated himself, and when he did I put two and two together in an unsettling way. I decided these rent-a-cops were going to teach Timmy some kind of lesson, maybe rough him up a little bit, so I did what any self-respecting idiot teammate would do in just this situation. I reached back and clocked the guy who seemed to have it in for Timmy—a world-class sucker punch that knocked him flat. A right—my pitching hand! Of course, as soon as I connected, I realized that the moment had gotten away from me. There was no way I could take on all of these cops, no way this unfortunate exchange could tilt our way.

As it happened, we were leaving Cooter's with Bobby Ojeda and Rick Aguilera, and the four of us were meaning to share a cab, so as long as I was being an idiot I just assumed that's what we would do here on in. Bobby and Rick didn't move—they were standing stock-still, unable to make sense of the senselessness that was happening in front of them. The two of them hadn't done anything except stand in exactly the wrong place at exactly the wrong time alongside exactly the wrong pair of teammates. And Timmy, he hadn't done anything except down a few too many and look to bend a couple of local ordinances. But me, I was the one who'd crossed some kind of line, and as I gamely tried to step back to the side of right I didn't get very far. I only took a couple of steps toward the cab before two of the cops grabbed me from behind, turned me around, and threw me toward the exterior wall of the club. Unfortunately, it was a spot of the wall that just happened to feature a plate glass window, and I went sailing right through it—just like in one of those old Hollywood oaters, I was thrown back through the window, into the saloon. (No Clint Eastwood moment for me—I wasn't thrown *out*, I was thrown back *in*.) The glass shattered into a million tiny pieces, so I calmly picked myself up off the nightclub floor, picked the shards of glass from my clothes, and headed back outside, like this sort of thing happened all the time.

There must have been a beat or two in there that I can no longer account for in the beery eye of memory, because the next thing I knew all these other cops had descended on the scene and they were arresting Timmy and Bobby and Rick ... and me. That's how it works in one of these dustups: arrest everyone and sort it out later. It makes it so there are no witnesses; we're all slogging through the same shit. Bobby can't say, "The guy threatened to break Teufel's arm before Darling hit him." Rick can't say, "The cops were baiting them." They can only lawyer up and head downtown—and, besides, I don't think Bobby or Rick even heard the menacing crap. Timmy didn't hear it, either. But there was no mistaking it for what it was, and even if I hadn't been sure I'd heard the guy the first time he had found a reason to repeat himself before I hit him.

Break his arm, he's with the Mets!

First call we made—the *only* call, really—was to the team's traveling secretary, Arthur Richman. Arthur, a former sportswriter, ended up as a vice president with the Yankees a couple of years later—he was the guy who famously convinced George Steinbrenner to hire Joe Torre as manager—but on this night in Houston he bailed us out and gave us a good talking to. It took awhile for him to get us out, though, so we spent most of the night in a small holding cell, just the four of us. It was early morning by the time we were released, and those wee hours passed like molasses. If one of us had a harmonica, we could have done a mean jailhouse version of "Nobody Knows the Trouble I've Seen."

We didn't talk much, as I recall. Whatever piss and vinegar Timmy and I had going in quickly passed through our systems, and Bobby and Rick were wondering what the hell they had done to find themselves in this particular mess. Mostly, my thoughts ran to my parents—I hated that I'd embarrassed them in this way. (Oh, and I kept checking my hand, opening and closing my fist, trying to figure out how I'd managed to throw a knockout punch without hurting myself, hoping like crazy I hadn't jeopardized my next start.) On a personal level,

I didn't regret my actions, so you could just forget about me showing any remorse, but I did regret the way my actions reflected on my family. My parents didn't deserve any of the negative press attention that would surely come their way. That off-duty cop, though—he got what he deserved, far as I was concerned. He was talking shit, and looking to trip us up, and threatening Timmy. I wasn't proud that I'd hit a cop, but I was proud that I'd stood up for my friend, even though Timmy had no idea what went down until after we got out of there.

For years, the four of us didn't talk about that night—not to each other at least. And yet for the rest of the season it dogged us. For the rest of our careers, in some ways, it dogged us. The Mets, to their great credit (and to my great surprise), stood behind us as an organization. Nobody in the front office gave us shit; they gave it a boys-will-be-boys spin when the press came calling. Davey Johnson didn't call us out or dress us down—not even in his backhanded, passive-aggressive way. About the only grief we got internally was from our own teammates, who got to the visiting clubhouse well ahead of us that day and decorated our lockers with black tape to make them look like jail cells. (Funny, right?)

Still, that night was a stain on our season. It fed whatever bad-boy reputation we'd been nursing all along, and set it up so that whenever we pulled into town for a series the local papers could get in their little potshot digs. The Mets hired a local criminal defense attorney to represent us—a guy named Dick DeGuerin, who would later go on to defend House majority leader Tom DeLay on money laundering charges, and cult leader David Koresh following his standoff with FBI and ATF agents in Waco, Texas. The deal was the Mets retained him, but his fee would be deducted from our salaries, and DeGuerin took up the argument that police officers should not be allowed to moonlight as bouncers. That was his whole defense, and he was confident we'd be cleared. He kept saying, "If you fight this to the end, nothing's gonna happen."

But DeGuerin scared the shit out of me. He was an amazing lawyer, determined to make his mark on this case, but I needed to get my head on straight and focus on the season. I knew this guy would get me off, but at what cost? I'd hit a police officer—there was no denying that. So in the end I pled no contest and waited for this thing to go away.

It was the story of our season, framed by those two giant flower boxes in front of Cooter's. It was how we played the game. We were bigger than the rules. Nothing could touch us. We were a team of destiny.

What the hell we were destined *for* . . . well, that was still anybody's guess.

SENTRY SUPER (supermarket chain): First kid to go with the flat-brimmed hat.

(Courtesy of Ron Darling)

Eleven-years old with the Millbury All-Stars in 1972. *(Courtesy of Ron Darling)*

WITH MY BROTHERS: Eddie, Brian, and Charlie.   *(Courtesy of Ron Darling)*

Does anyone take a good high school photo? I didn't in 1978. St. John Pioneers, Shrewsbury, Massachusetts.
(Courtesy of Yale University)

BULLDOG: The sports-publicity department at Yale didn't have to tell me how to pose for this promo shot. I'd spent countless hours with my brothers, mimicking the baseball-card images of big-league pitchers, so I had the look down. *(Courtesy of Yale University)*

FEELING HITTERISH: A lot of pitchers will tell you their favorite thing to do is swing the bat in a big spot. Here I am taking a cut for Yale. I'd like to report here that I drove this pitch to the gap in left-center—so I'll go ahead and do just that.   *(Courtesy of Yale University)*

RON DARLING

I loved finishing my career in Oakland, although it took a while to get used to pitching in those white shoes.
(Courtesy of Yale University)

YOUNG GUN: My first spring training camp with the Mets. *(Getty Images)*

BAND OF BROTHERS: I've come to look forward to these round-number anniversaries. Here we are gathered at Shea for the twentieth anniversary of our 1986 championship season. It's tough to look at this shot and be reminded that Gary Carter and Frank Cashen are no longer with us—in many ways, the two of them were the head and heart of that team. *(Getty Images)*

A HELLUVA TOWN: This was our view as we made our way up the Canyon of Heroes for the ticker-tape parade. (Note the actual ticker tape!) *(Getty Images)*

A WINNING TEAM: In the booth with my friends and colleagues Gary Cohen and Keith Hernandez, my broadcast partners at SNY and WPIX-TV. When we call a game together, it's like we're kicking back around a big-screen television over beers—only without the beers. *(Courtesy of Ron Darling)*

6

THINGS FALL APART

Nobody said anything to me when I got back to the dugout in the middle of the first inning. That's how it goes in these big games—in success, in struggle, your teammates steer clear. I might have tried to convince myself I was pitching from a place of confidence, but the guys could see I was nervous so they gave me even more room than usual, only you didn't have to watch me pitch to know I was tense. You could see it in the way I moved, the way I bit my lip, the way I covered my face with my glove.

Corner of my eye, I could see Davey Johnson huddled with Mel Stottlemyre at the other end of the dugout. Those two were always talking, comparing notes, strategizing. I had a pretty good idea how that conversation was going, and every reason to think I was its main subject. (What *else* were they going to talk about?) Davey was probably saying, "How's he lookin', Mel? Has he got it today?"

Mel was probably thinking he could lie, or tell the truth,

or land somewhere in between, but I'm betting he leaned my way. On a team with a pitcher-resistant (pitcher-*allergic*?) manager, there's a curious dugout dynamic. Always, the pitching coach has a lot invested in his starters; his job rides on ours, and this was especially so with Mel, so he was inclined to give us the benefit of the doubt if we got off to a rough start. He could point to our body of work to justify his confidence. He could say something like, "He's a little jumpy, but why wouldn't he be? He'll settle down. He'll be fine."

But I wasn't fine, not yet. Looking back on that rocky first inning, it's clear to me I was thinking too much, overthrowing. In the moment, I don't think I knew any such thing. All I knew was there'd been a bunch of hard-hit balls; my fastball was flat, straight; my stomach was in knots. And yet even with all of that, I was glad to have gotten through that first inning, told myself it was a character-builder, a sigh of relief, a thing to get past; told myself I'd still managed to put a zero on the board and that I was now set up to come back out in the top of the second with a little something else on the ball.

One of the great equalizers for a pitcher is a cushion, so right away I started thinking how we might put some runs on the board in the bottom of the first. There's nothing like a three-run lead, early, to help a pitcher settle in and find his game. Also, it helped to remind myself that the butterflies were not my own; they were everywhere and all around. Whatever tension I was feeling, however big this game had loomed in my head, I kept reminding myself it was just as tense, just as big for Bruce Hurst, my opposite number. (Probably, it was just as big for everyone in uniform that night at Shea—in both dugouts.) So, there was that. If we could get to Hurst, I could relax, find my rhythm. He'd strung up a bunch of zeroes in this series, same as me; he'd pitched a bunch of innings, same as me. We were trading punches, dead even. The key difference, really, was that Bruce Hurst hadn't had that extra day to wrap his head around this game, an extra day of weight and worry, and I had to think this gave him an edge.

Remember, Dennis "Oil Can" Boyd was originally scheduled to start Game 7 for the Red Sox. The rainout the day before now meant an extra day of rest for John McNamara's ace, so Hurst was able to step in and turn our lineup around, since Davey Johnson deployed a fairly strict righty-lefty platoon in center and at second base. I tried not to let this switch play with my head, but it did, in subtle ways. Going into the game, I thought we were giving up something defensively with Mookie Wilson in center instead of Lenny Dykstra, and with Tim Teufel at second instead of Wally Backman. Nothing against my friends Mookie and Timmy, but Lenny covered a little more ground; Wally was a little more sure-handed. On balance, it felt to me like we were a little more explosive at the top of the order with Lenny and Wally hitting one and two—but I wasn't being paid to set the lineup.

(Lately, Davey had folded our most-everyday left fielder Kevin Mitchell into his platoon mix, sliding the switch-hitting Mookie to left and leaving Lenny to roam center field.)

Going into the bottom of the first, I now started to realize, we were giving up something at the plate as well. I hadn't let myself get this far in my thinking until just this moment.

My focus had been on the Boston lineup, not ours. But now that it felt to me we needed to push a run across so I could breathe a little easier on the mound, I was thinking with a bat in my hands. Lenny had been one of our hottest hitters down the stretch, in the playoffs, in the World Series. He'd gotten that sweet leadoff triple in Game 6 against Houston off lefty Bob Knepper to start the ninth inning rally that sent that game into extra innings—a game we ended up winning in the sixteenth inning to take the series—so it's not like he couldn't hit left-handed pitching in a big spot. Truth was, Bruce Hurst didn't throw hard enough to bother a left-handed hitter like Lenny, not with the way he'd been swinging the bat. But we'd ridden those platoons all the way to this Game 7, the end of the line, and Davey Johnson knew full well that Mookie Wilson and Timmy Teufel were two of the key reasons we'd won 108 games in the regular season.

Baseball is a game of percentages, tendencies, and here we were playing the odds of a long season over nine innings. Davey's moves made a whole lot of sense on paper, in theory, but I worried they didn't make as much sense on this particular night, on this particular field. We were playing a percentage game instead of a momentum game, it seemed to me just then. I thought of these things, these subtle differences to our lineup, as Mookie stepped to the plate to take his licks—only, he took just one lick. He swung at the very first pitch, grounding out to second and putting a serious dent in our chances of rattling Bruce Hurst right out of the gate.

Here again, this is not a knock on Mookie—that's just the way he played. Typically, you want your leadoff hitter to work the pitcher a bit to start the game, see what he has. You want to give your own pitcher a chance to sit his butt down, regroup. But Mookie had never been that kind of hitter; you could almost see him start to swing the bat as he climbed the dugout steps. He was an aggressive hitter, an aggressive base runner. Would I have liked to see him take a few pitches in this situation? Absolutely, but that was just me, taking a selfish view. That was just me wanting Bruce Hurst to work as hard in his first inning as I'd had to work in mine. I wanted him to sweat a little bit. I wanted him to overthink things. And Mookie probably understood this on an intellectual level because he was a great student of the game, but I have to think he was a little nervous, too. That's what a Game 7 can do to you—there are jitters all around. Some of those jitters make their way into the box score, but most of them don't.

Even the home plate umpire John Kibler was nervous, jumpy, *off* on a couple of calls. That's just how it goes on a big stage. It takes awhile to find your game.

As Mookie came back into the dugout, I put myself in Bruce Hurst's cleats. To him, an at bat like that to start the game was like a gift from the baseball gods. One pitch, one out—that's one of the most euphoric feelings for a starting pitcher. It almost never happens that way, and when it does it's as if you've won the lottery. You really haven't done anything yet. You haven't established anything, you haven't sequenced any pitches, and you've already got an out. It's awesome, and just then I hated that we'd allowed him to feel even the tiniest bit awesome in this early going.

In this way, I realized Hurst's *sigh of relief* was far different from mine. His relief was like finding a crisp fifty-dollar bill on the sidewalk; mine was like losing that same fifty and snatching it back just before some asshole put it in his pocket and walked away.

Teufel was next, and I caught myself thinking he could catch Hurst feeling a little too comfortable, a little too flush with the gift he'd just been given, maybe drive a hanging curve for extra bases. A lot of folks forget that Timmy had a lot of pop in his bat—really, he had tremendous power for a guy his size. First time I'd ever seen him play was in the Cape Cod league, where he was a home run champion, and of course he'd set all kinds of records at Clemson, where he'd played college ball. But Timmy could only manage a nothing pop-up on a 2-2 pitch to second baseman Marty Barrett—another gift for Bruce Hurst.

With two out, Keith Hernandez strode to the plate in the three hole, and I took the time to appreciate his approach. Now, a part of me hates how I've just fallen back on such an easy baseball cliché: *strode* is the fallback action verb of the lazy play-by-play man, running out of ways to describe a batter's walk from the on-deck circle to the batter's box. But here I believe it applies—surely, the coinage came about with Keith in mind. Surely, in cliché, there is occasional truth. Consider: Keith would always take three hard practice swings before digging in, inching ever closer to the plate with each cut, looking more and more ready and on top of his game. He *strode*, let's be clear. There was purpose in his approach. It was the kind of thing you don't really notice until someone points it out to you—like background music that doesn't register until you start hearing it over and over. It was almost like an OCD thing with Keith, a way to clear his head. Three hard swings, each and every time. You see this type of behavior in a lot of athletes. We all have our quirks and tics and rigid superstitions, and here Keith was just putting himself through these familiar paces, dialing in, reaching for consistency, *striding* . . . doing everything he could to make sure he was mentally and physically prepared for battle. A routine like that, it's especially helpful in a big game because it sets it up like any other at bat. It could be an August night in Pittsburgh, or Game 7 of the World Series.

As a pitcher, I didn't reach for any of these patterns— maybe I should have. I could have windmilled my arms a certain way, toed the rubber a certain way, tugged the bill of my cap . . . anything just to get me to stay loose, focused. When I was in trouble, when I was overthrowing, I used to step off and stretch my arms as a way to tell myself to calm the fuck down. But here I could only admire Keith's professionalism. His *precision*. To him, it was just another at bat. Nothing could rattle him—nothing, that is, except for the planes flying overhead in and out of LaGuardia. Oh, man, that used to piss him off, and here he stepped out with the count 1-0, a low-flying jet announcing its arrival, and you could see him look to the sky, shake his head, try to regain his focus.

On a 1-1 pitch, Keith crushed a ball to dead center, right at Dave Henderson, who took a couple steps in to make the catch for the third out, so the only positive we could take with us onto the field was that Keith had hit the ball hard. For Keith, this was as much a negative as a positive, because he was pissed that he'd hit the ball right to Henderson's glove. But for the rest of the team, it told us we could hit this guy. We'd been pretty much stymied in Hurst's first two starts, but this could be our night.

Maybe, *just* maybe, we could get to him.

I took my time getting back to the mound—guess I was more like Keith Hernandez than I thought, because I had my own little warm-up rituals, my own little idiosyncrasies. I always threw eight pitches: four fastballs—two outside, two inside—two curveballs, one fork ball, one from the stretch, send it down. Eight felt like a good number, so that was my thing. Before the first inning, I allowed myself a little wiggle room. Most nights, I'd throw these same eight warm-up pitches to start the game, but if I threw the first two and something didn't feel right, I'd start in again. I'd allow myself a couple more fastballs, wasn't so rigid in my count.

After that, the eight count was sacrosanct—only here it wasn't enough to fill the break between innings. Why? Because during the World Series the network layered in an extra chunk of time to sell commercials. I didn't want to be out there waiting after I'd completed my warm-ups, and I didn't want to add to my warm-up pitch count, so I let my teammates take the field and get going on their own rituals before I got going on mine. It was all about the timing, and I'd already had a couple of postseason starts to get it down.

Dwight Evans was due to lead off the inning, and he was a tough, workmanlike hitter—smart, quick, efficient. Along with Jim Rice, he was one of the through-lines that ran all the way back to that great Red Sox team that made it to Game 7 of the 1975 World Series, so he'd been around. (And from there, you could find a couple of through-lines to the Impossible Dream team of 1967, with Yaz and Rico Petrocelli.) He'd been in this spot before, wasn't likely to shrink from it.

I knew Evans had just seen me throw nothing but fastballs the entire first inning, so I started him off with a breaking ball, just to mix it up, give him a different look. Trouble was, I was still throwing too hard, reaching, so the ball was high and outside—not even close. Still, Gary Carter wanted me to come back with another breaking ball at this point, but I shook him off. I'd missed so big with that first pitch, I didn't want to risk going down 2-0 to such a solid hitter, so I came back with a fastball that Evans fouled off to even the count at 1-1. He fouled off the next one, too, and for the first time all game I started to feel like I was dictating an at bat. Whatever rhythm I'd been missing in the top of the first seemed to find me here in the second, so I went from feeling down and tentative to up and confident in the space of just three pitches.

That's how it goes out there on the mound—the loneliest place in team sports. You talk yourself onto a ledge for no good reason, and then you talk yourself back down for no good reason. Somehow, in all that climbing and clambering, you are meant to find your way.

Next, at 1-2, I came back with a hard sinker at the knees that should have been a called strike three, but John Kibler thought it was a ball. That's baseball, right? In the stands, in the booth, in the *dugout,* even, you learn to roll with the calls that go against you. But on the mound, in the middle of a big moment, you don't roll so easy. Anyway, *I* didn't roll so easy. I wanted that pitch, earned that pitch, fought for that pitch, and the fact that I didn't get the call . . . well, it was deflating. I liked John Kibler, thought he was a tremendous umpire, but here I think this was one of those instances when his own big-game jitters clouded his thinking. It was a good pitch, but the call went the other way, and on the back of that one call I went from feeling like I was in control to feeling like the at bat was slipping away from me. And it was. I shouldn't have let it, but this was my inexperience on full display. This was me, not being ready for this big moment.

This was me, rattled.

The line between dominating and being dominated can be paper-thin, and this one missed call pushed me across it. I took a little extra time before the next pitch—in part to let John Kibler know I wasn't happy with the call, and in part to check my emotions. Really, it messed with my game plan—not just for this one hitter, but for the entire game. If the home plate umpire wasn't going to give me that call, it was going to be a long night. As far as Dwight Evans, leading off this second inning, was concerned, it was looking like it was going to be a long at bat. A lot of times, you use the whole at bat to set up a hitter, get him looking, leaning one way, and then you execute your pitch, only here I'd set up Evans and worked him just right and still didn't get the call. It messed with my head, knocked me off my game.

I came back with a split-finger in just about the same spot, but Evans fouled it off to keep the count at 2-2. This was potentially a problem—me, coming back to the same spot—but for the time being this was my approach. Then I missed big with a fastball inside to run the count full. At this point, I was reeling—fuming, actually. I couldn't let the Red Sox see it, and I didn't want to show up John Kibler, but it felt to me as though I'd had this batter and now he was getting away from me. Evans should have been punched out on that 1-2 pitch at the knees. I'd set him up perfectly, but by now he'd seen two more pitches than he should have seen. Two more pitches to take my measure, two more pitches to get comfortable, two more pitches to wait me out, see if I would make a mistake.

Evans fouled off the next pitch, too—a high pop-up that tailed out of play down the first-base line—so as he dug in for the eighth pitch of the at bat, four more than he was probably entitled to, he'd given himself an edge. He'd seen me scramble to erase John Kibler's call. He'd seen me go to the well, try to pitch him inside. He'd seen that sinker at the knees. He'd seen my changeup, even if it wasn't a very good one. He'd seen just about everything I had to throw at him—and, worst of all, he'd seen me rattled. It's tough to make a veteran hitter miss, tough to jam him four times in the same at bat, but that's just what I tried to do on the next pitch. It felt to me like I had no choice—only, Dwight Evans didn't miss. He waited on that next pitch—a fastball, inside, at the knees—and timed it just right and sent the ball sailing over the wall in deep left-center.

I knew it was gone the moment he hit it. If you watch the replay, you can see my shoulders sag at the crack of the bat. You can see my head drop. I didn't even turn to watch the ball clear the fence. I just waited for Evans to round the bases and get the hell off the field.

Now, I'd given up a ton of home runs in my career, and for the most part when you get beat like that you find a way to shrug it off and move on. You roll with it, same way you do with a bad call—at least, that's the idea. But on this night, on this grand stage, under just these circumstances, it wasn't so easy to set it aside. It was just one lousy run, the game barely under way, nothing we couldn't recover from and yet it gnawed at me, the way this at bat had slipped away. I was in control, and then I wasn't; down from the ledge and then back on. I'd had Dwight Evans just where I wanted him, and then I didn't. And it all came apart on the back of that one missed call.

So what did I do? I kicked the dirt and sucked it up and tried to compose myself. There was nothing else to do, really. There was still a game to be played, and the next batter I was meant to play it with was my lifelong nemesis Rich Gedman. We had a history, going back over ten years, only the Richie Gedman I was facing in the World Series looked nothing like the Richie Gedman I used to face in high school. He was a totally different hitter. Walt Hriniak had been working with him, tinkering with his stance, his swing. Gedman and Evans were both Hriniak disciples, and when they dug in to face me they looked like mirror images of each other—crouched low, bat back, a ton of movement as they waited on the pitch. The Richie Gedman I used to face in high school was one of the most natural hitters I'd ever seen; he had a pure, fluid swing. I used to hate going up against him.

I started Geddie off with a fastball low and away. I wanted to get a good look at him before putting a ball over the plate, and I wasn't about to get beat on back-to-back pitches, so in a lot of ways it was a wasted pitch, something to get out of the way. He fouled off the next pitch with that big, looping swing of his, bringing the count even at 1-1. Then my luck turned against me for the second time in this inning, as Gedman grounded the next pitch foul down the first-base line. This alone wasn't unlucky—it put me ahead in the count, 1-2—but what happened as a result of that foul grounder had me reeling, fuming all over again. A couple of fans leaned over the railing behind first base, hoping to scoop up the ball as it bounced their way. Here again, that's baseball, right? Fans are always reaching for foul balls—only here, the weight of all these fans pressed against the portable stands knocked the temporary fence right to the ground. I didn't really see what happened, but when I turned to face the commotion on that side of the field I could see a dozen or so people splayed in the dirt, about thirty feet of fencing knocked on its face, the bunting all bunched on the ground, security guards and grounds crew members hurrying to survey the scene. It was almost surreal, to have to take this in, at just this moment, in just this way, so I turned away from it, tried to put it out of my mind and focus on Gedman. Trouble was, it took a good long while for the grounds crew to set the fence back in place and for play to resume, and in that long while I found the time to get myself worked up all over again.

Perhaps I overstate, suggesting that I was fuming over this delay. But I was certainly irritated, distracted. I caught myself thinking I was playing for some rinky-dink minor league operation, instead of a major league baseball club in the seventh game of a World Series. (I'm sure some of today's pitchers feel the same way about the umpire reviews that have crept into the game.) I cursed the Mets and Major League Baseball for adding those extra folding seats along the right- and left-field lines. Everyone else on that field and in those stands was able to laugh about this, marvel that nobody had been hurt, find a way to fill the time until we could start back up again, but to me it was unsettling. It must have been unsettling to Rich

Gedman, too, but I wasn't too worried about his ability to focus.

In all, it took a little less than four minutes for the wall to be secured, the fans reseated, the bunting hung back in place, but that was more than enough time for me to lose my rhythm, more than enough time to take me out of my game—but it would turn out to be the best "time-out" in Boston sports history. During the delay, I took a few warm-up pitches, tried to stay loose, focused, but this kind of thing just doesn't happen so I had no framework for it. Like I said, it was unsettling—so unsettling that Gedman stroked the very next pitch over the wall in right-center field, just off the glove of Darryl Strawberry, the tallest player on the field. (Guess it wasn't such a big deal to Richie, huh?) At 6'6", Darryl had a shot at it, and in fact it looked for a beat or two in there like he'd made the grab. From his body language, it appeared in a flash that Darryl himself thought he'd come down with the ball, but just like that we were down 2–0 and I was on my heels.

Two pitches—two *lousy* pitches—each thrown from a place of disadvantage.

Now, there's one thing I must make clear: I was never a whiner, never really cared for whiners. To bend that great Tom Hanks line from *A League of Their Own,* there's no whining in baseball. The calls are the calls. The breaks of the game are the breaks of the game. But as an analyst, revisiting the biggest game of my career from the perspective of thirty years, it's hard not to notice the sequence of events set in motion by these two unlucky moments. I don't set them out as an excuse for my subpar performance that night at Shea but as a way to place that subpar performance in context. This is what happened. And this is what happened next. The one followed from the other.

As a twenty-six-year-old pitcher with three years of major league experience, I don't think I even recognized how the game might have turned on the prolonged Evans at bat, on the rickety fencing. Already, I'd struggled a bit in that first inning, so who can say how the game would have gone? But after a lifetime in the game, I like to think it would have gone some other way.

Meanwhile, I still had to get out of the inning—and here on in, I didn't make things any easier.

I walked the next batter, Dave Henderson, which of course brought Mel Stottlemyre to the mound. He had nothing to say to me, really. He was just buying time so Davey could get a pitcher up in the bullpen, and I knew in this early going that the pitcher he'd tap would most likely be Sid Fernandez, who was rested and good to go. A game like this, the season on the line, your starting pitcher is on a short leash, and here I'd stretched the hell out of mine. Any other game, those back-to-back home runs might have been dismissed as a hiccup, a bother, but here on the precipice of a world championship they were huge.

The thing about these trips to the mound was there was never all that much to say. I mean, what could Mel have told me that I didn't already know? *Hey, Ronnie, try not to give up any more home runs, okay?* The visit was rarely about strategy and it was only sometimes about motivation, picking me up. Mostly, it was a way to call a time-out, take my pulse. Mel wanted to see how I was holding up, see what he could learn about my demeanor. And me, I just wanted him to turn and head right back to the dugout so I could get back to my job—a job I wasn't doing all that well. He was out there for just a few moments, can't remember what we talked about, but I do remember that the whole time I kept thinking like a golfer. Like a lot of athletes, I was a perfectionist, and this game was far from perfect, so I found myself wishing for a Mulligan—you know, a way to start over, pretend those two lousy pitches never happened. But I'd already sent my tee shot into the woods, and I would have to play it where it lay.

Spike Owen loomed as a point of pause in the Red Sox lineup. He was a professional hitter, capable of doing damage, hitting over .350 in the series heading into this game, but he was also a light-hitting shortstop. I chose to dwell on the *light-hitting shortstop* part and pitched to his résumé instead of his hot bat, got ahead of him 0-2. Frankly, I was more concerned with Dave Henderson at first base than I was with Spike Owen at the plate. If I wasn't careful, Henderson could steal his way into scoring position and make an even bigger mess out of this inning, so I threw over to first before coming home, just to keep the base runner honest. In those days, the coaching staff didn't micromanage those throws to first the way they do today. We developed our own feel for that part of the game, and here my feeling was that Henderson was itching to run. I threw over a second time, at 0-2, before coaxing Spike Owen to poke a lazy pop fly to Rafael Santana at short for the first out of the inning.

The pitcher's spot was next in the order, and the book told me Bruce Hurst wasn't much of a hitter. But I didn't need the book in this case: I'd struck out Hurst three straight times when I faced him in Game 1, left him looking a little wobbly at the plate. However, the book also told me that he'd be sacrificing in this spot, so I couldn't go after him in the same way. I'd have to bust him inside, make his life difficult, instead of trying to make him miss.

I had a routine worked out with Keith Hernandez for just this situation. I'd throw twice to first base and then throw a pitch to the plate. Keith was probably the most aggressive first baseman in the history of the game—certainly, the most aggressive I'd ever seen—and he liked to get a good jump on the ball and sprint toward home as I went into my motion, hoping to cut off a bunt down the first-base line in time to make a play at second base. It was a thing to see, his fearless, peerless dash toward the batter. From time to time, he'd make it all the way to the batter's box, or just about, and after a while you started seeing other first basemen around the league taking the same aggressive approach. It changed the game, the way he defended against the sacrifice, and it was one of the great thrills of my career to be a small part of that change, but on this night we went another way, thinking the Boston scouts had surely figured us out on this. Keith actually came to the mound for a little strategy session as Hurst stepped to the plate, and we decided to go after him immediately, maybe catch Henderson a little flat-footed at first.

So there was Keith, mad-dashing toward home, intimidating the hell out of Bruce Hurst, and on the third-base side Ray Knight was doing his version of the same thing—a little less aggressive, perhaps, but still charging pretty hard. Sure enough, Hurst pushed the ball to the left side of the infield, but Ray Knight was coming so hard he sailed right past the ball as he tried to one-hand it with his glove. It might have been a bad bounce off the wet field after all that rain the day before, or it might have been that Ray was having some big-game jitters of his own, but it worked out that I was in place to collect the ball and fire down to Timmy Teufel covering first in time for the out, so there was no harm on the play—except maybe to our team ego.

At this point in the game, down a couple of runs, the world on the line, you start making little deals with yourself on the mound. You tell yourself that if you get out of this inning with no further damage your teammates still have a shot. You tell yourself this wasn't how you wanted to start the game, but now that you're in this spot you'll find a way to make the best of it, hang in there, refuse to back down. You tell yourself that next time, if there ever is a next time, you'll take the hill for Game 7 of the World Series with a different swagger, a different approach. You come up with all these different if/then scenarios, but the *if* is the same in all of them: *if* you stop the bleeding, you're still in this thing; *if* you strand Henderson on second, you can come back in the bottom of the inning with the heart of your lineup and start chipping away at the lead; *if* you find your groove, here on in, you'll put up a bunch of zeroes until your teammates find a way to get to Hurst and take the lead. Absolutely, you've dug a hole, but it's not so big you can't climb out of it yet, so you reach back for a little something extra so you can get back to the dugout and regroup.

The only trouble with this approach was that I'd yet to start pitching. I'd gone all the way through the Boston lineup, thrown more than forty pitches, most of them fastballs. Really, there was no *pitching* going on, only *throwing*. No, I didn't think just then that I could *throw* my way through the Boston lineup a second time, so I put a ton of pressure on myself as Wade Boggs came to the plate. If Henderson had gotten on some other way, if he'd hit the ball hard instead of working out a walk, we might have thought of putting Boggs on with an intentional walk, with two outs and first base open. But I'd handled Boggs pretty well the entire series, so we decided to pitch to him. First time around, he'd hit the ball hard, lining out to Santana at short, and I had to think he'd been studying me ever since. You don't get to be one of the best pure hitters in the game by just stepping to the plate and taking your chances. Take that approach and you might catch a break a time or two, do some damage, but you won't hit .357 over the course of a season, so there was no fooling Wade Boggs. He was probably guessing that I'd start him out with a breaking ball, since I hadn't really featured it, hadn't had much success with my fastball, so I started him out with a sinker that caught the outside corner. Then I came back inside to push him off the plate. At 1-1, I wasted one away, and followed it up with another sinker that caught that same outside corner to even the count at 2-2. Before each pitch, I looked Henderson back at second, tried to keep him close, but the reality was that we were playing Boggs to pull, so Teufel was too far off the bag to really bird-dog the runner at second.

Two balls, two strikes, two out, two runs in . . . Boggs finally caught a piece of a breaking ball low and away and poked it up the middle, just past the reach of a diving Santana, and Henderson came around to score. A professional hitter like Boggs, he was probably sitting on that breaking ball. It was a good pitch, but it wasn't good enough—and here again it came down to me giving these good hitters too many looks at the same thing. Dwight Evans had seen four pitches in the same area before taking me deep, and now Wade Boggs had had two at bats and seen five pitches low and away, so this was just poor pitching on my part.

Like I said, I was just throwing. I wasn't mixing up my speeds, wasn't mixing up my location—it just wasn't a very good game plan: sinkers down and in to righties, down and away to lefties. It was a game plan that put us down three runs—a hole of entirely different dimensions.

I'd taken all those if/then scenarios and sent them to re-write, and now here was Marty Barrett digging in with a shovel in his hands. Remember, this was the hottest hitter in the Boston lineup, he seemed to will his way on base the entire series, so I naturally assumed he'd be looking to put a good swing on the ball, maybe push across another run. So what did he do? He laid down a picture-perfect *swatting* bunt—the ball fairly hugged the tall grass along the third-base line and ran out of steam before Ray Knight could get to it and pick it up. Barrett couldn't have *placed* the ball any better.

That bunt caught us completely by surprise, I'll say that. It was an odd play. In a lot of ways, it was a selfish play. Ray Knight was playing deep, so Barrett knew if he executed he could reach first safely. But all he was doing was passing the baton to Bill Buckner, putting the burden on the next guy in the order to do the real damage—the kind of play that doesn't always endear yourself to your teammates. Yeah, he kept the rally going; yeah, he put another runner on base; but he had to take the bat out of his own hands to do so.

The bunt brought Buckner back to the plate, and I had to think he was looking to swing at the first pitch, keep the pressure on, so I was careful to place the ball wide, just out of reach. Then, on the very next pitch, Buckner must have known I'd come back to that down and away sweet spot; he drove a ball to deep left-center that Mookie Wilson was able to run down, but only because he got a great jump. Without that jump, the ball could have fallen over Mookie's head for a double, and Boggs and Barrett could have tiptoed home with another two killing runs, so as Mookie trotted in with the ball I caught myself thinking things could have been worse.

Oh, things were miserable enough, down 3–0 in the biggest game of my career, but they could have been far worse. The walls had come down on my World Series, *literally*, if you counted the collapse of the temporary fencing on that Gedman grounder, and I could only hope there was time enough for us to build them back up again.

PUT ME OUT, PUT ME OUT, PUT ME OUT OF MISERY

There is nothing like the sound of 50,032 boisterous, thrill-happy fans leaking from a rickety old building on a chilly October night. In just about a half hour, Shea Stadium had gone from a rollicking funhouse, a raucous din of furious noise that seemed about to drown out the planes flying overhead, to a kind of tomb. Where there was once joy and abandon and hope and infectious enthusiasm and all those good things there was now gloom and doom, almost like somebody had died—and whoever it was, it felt to me like I'd killed him.

It is difficult to overstate the stunned silence that seemed to wash over the Shea crowd—and into that stunned silence I imagined every invective, every expletive, every snide comment being mumbled under every breath with me in mind. Mets fans were respectful enough—and, I suppose, *innocent* enough—that I didn't hear too many boos as I walked off the field after that disastrous second inning, but that didn't mean 50,032 people weren't thinking about giving me the biggest

raspberry the game had ever seen. That didn't mean the boo-
ing wasn't implied. I could *feel* the boos, sense the disappointment all around.

Here again, my teammates gave me a wide berth when I
got back to the dugout, and this was just as well with me. I
didn't want to talk to anybody. I was like a kid who'd misbe-
haved and been sent to the corner to *think about what he'd
done,* only here that was precisely what the situation called for.
I needed to be by myself, off to the side, alone with my thoughts
in a raspberry-free vacuum, to work the situation over in my
mind, find a way to get my head right and start solving those
Red Sox hitters before they were done solving me. The moment had gotten away from me—the *biggest* moment of my
career!—and I wanted desperately to take it back, but the only
way to do that was to hang in there until my teammates could
reclaim the three runs I'd just donated to the other side. And
the *hang in there* part was crucial, because it felt to me like I
still had something to prove.

Oh, you better believe I had something to prove, but I had
no idea if I could stick around long enough to do so. As a
pitcher, the manager gives you the ball, but it's never really out
of his hands. I hadn't exactly given Davey Johnson a whole lot
of reasons to keep me in the game. Already, Sid Fernandez had
been up and down in the bullpen. Already, Mel Stottlemyre
had been out to the mound to take my pulse. Already, I could
see the wheels turning in Davey's head as he tried to calculate
the precise point of diminishing returns on my lackluster
start, to survey the depths of the hole I'd just dug for him.

Gary Carter led off the bottom of the second for us, and
here Kid seemed to want to borrow a page from the Boston

playbook, slapping a surprise bunt to the third-base side on the first pitch of the inning. Like the Marty Barrett bunt in the top half of the inning, it was an unusual move. Kid was our cleanup hitter, after all, so everyone in the ballpark was expecting him to swing away, but he was a savvy player, knew he couldn't erase that three-run lead with one swing of the bat, knew we needed base runners, thought he might catch the Red Sox napping. And he nearly did—except for Bruce Hurst, who made an excellent play to nip Carter at first.

Still, for the second time in two innings, our leadoff hitter was retired on just one pitch, and after Darryl Strawberry lofted a high fly ball to left on a 1-0 count for the second out Hurst had thrown only a dozen pitches. By contrast—by *stark* contrast—I'd thrown fifty-one pitches, and of the six outs I'd managed to record, four were on hard-hit balls that could have fallen for extra bases and one was on a sacrifice. And so to this point, clearly, Hurst's outing could not have gone any better, while mine could not have gone any worse. I had only to look to the mound to see the differences in our demeanor; Hurst toed the rubber like there was no place on the planet he'd rather be, while I shifted uneasily at the edge of the dugout bench wishing I was anyplace else.

Apparently, I'd sucked so much air out of that stadium that when Ray Knight stroked a one-hop single up the middle with two outs in the second, the fans seemed to hardly take note. It's like they were too numb to stand and cheer. Normally, first hit of the game for the home team, there'd be a wave of excitement rolling through the crowd, but here there was hardly a ripple, nothing really to celebrate, and by the time Kevin Mitchell grounded weakly to first on a check swing to end the inning these small signs of life had been stilled yet again. It's like the crowd had been so beaten down by that 3–0 deficit, they'd already written us off.

Happily, incredibly, my teammates didn't take the same view. Up and down the bench, there was an unshakeable sense that this was still our game, our series, our time to shine. We were a confident, arrogant bunch, used to coming from behind, comfortable being counted out, and to a man everyone believed we would claw our way back into this thing. I believed this, too—hell, I *had* to believe this, else I would have hung my head so low it would have been flattened against the sluice of tobacco juice and sunflower seed husks strewn across the dugout floor. And so I told myself whatever I needed to tell myself as I walked back to the mound and tried to set right the pendulum—maybe find a way to get the momentum to swing back in our direction.

The problem with this plan was that Jim Rice was waiting for me in the batter's box, and he had me figured. He crushed a first-pitch curve ball to the left-field fence that looked for a long moment like it was going to leave the yard. Instead, it short-hopped the wall, but in that long moment I went from thinking I could set things right to thinking I might have thrown my last pitch. I was up and down and all over the damn place in my thinking. But then the ball seemed to bounce our way. Kevin Mitchell played the ball perfectly off the carom. As Rice rounded first and tried to stretch this thing into a double Kevin spun toward the infield and let fly with a one-hop bullet to Tim Teufel covering the bag to nail the sliding Red Sox slugger, bringing the crowd to its feet and shaking the doldrums from the Shea faithful—for the moment, at least.

It was, truly, a remarkable play, and a whole lot happened on the back of it. Also, a whole lot *didn't* happen, which in my narrow view was just as important. You see, for me, this remarkable play was a stay of execution. With Rice on second with a leadoff double, and two guys who'd already taken me deep in Evans and Gedman due up next, Davey Johnson would have surely yanked me at this point. Sid Fernandez had already warmed up, so he was probably ten pitches away from being ready to come into the game, but this one play kept me out there.

This one play gave me life, hope, and it put back some of the air I'd let out of the stadium.

A lot of folks forget about Kevin Mitchell when they look back at the 1986 Mets team, but he was an incredible athlete and one of the keys to our success in his rookie season. (He finished third in that year's Rookie of the Year voting, by the way.) He was also a great guy to have in the clubhouse, although management was quick to write him off because he was a tough kid from San Diego. He got into his share of trouble off the field, but he was one of my favorite teammates of all time. He was a hard guy to know, but there was a soft side to him—he used to cut a lot of guys' hair, although I never trusted a teammate around me with a pair of scissors. Kevin went on to win the National League MVP award in 1989 for the Giants, but we couldn't even find a spot for him in the lineup at the start of the 1986 season. We left spring training that year with George Foster as our starting left fielder—a lot of folks forget *that,* too. What they remember is that Foster had a tough time in New York, after a Hall of Fame-ish career with those great "Big Red Machine" teams from Cincinnati in the 1970s. For more than a decade, he was one of the most feared hitters in the game, but then he came to New York and could only put up mediocre numbers.

By the end of July, Davey Johnson was running out of ways to get Kevin Mitchell's bat into the lineup on a regular basis—he could play all three outfield positions, shortstop, third, and first, so Davey had a lot of options—and it was looking more and more like we'd be a stronger club if we swapped the rookie Mitchell for the veteran Foster, but the team had put a lot of money into George, pinned a lot of hopes on his arrival, and the Mets were careful to treat him with the respect he'd earned. Then a bench-clearing brawl (in Cincinnati, of all places!) helped to decide the issue. What happened was the Reds' fleet-footed center fielder Eric Davis stole third, and even though he was in safely he took offense at what he thought was a hard tag by Ray Knight. The two started jawing and, soon enough, jabbing. Both benches cleared, and a good, old-fashioned dustup ensued, but if you did a quick head count you would have seen that George Foster was the only Met to stay out of the melee. He remained on the bench throughout, and when he was asked about it later he said fighting set a bad example for young baseball fans. This may have been true, but *not fighting,* not having your teammates' backs, set a bad tone in the clubhouse, and soon after this incident Davey Johnson announced that Kevin Mitchell would be his everyday left fielder.

Whether the move followed from that brawl in Cincinnati, Davey never made clear—and from my experience, this was totally consistent with Davey's style of managing. He avoided confrontation, but made his feelings known in a sidelong way, and here there was no mistaking the message. Several weeks later George Foster was given his outright release and replaced on the roster by longtime fan favorite Lee Mazzilli, a homegrown talent who was once the matinee-idol face of the franchise. Once again, in the great circle of baseball life that envelops the game, Mazzilli's initial tour of duty in New York had been cut short at the start of the 1982 season when the Mets traded him to the Texas Rangers for a couple of young pitchers.

Those pitchers? Walt Terrell, who went on to win over 100 games in a peripatetic ten-year career that took him from New York, to Detroit, to San Diego, back to New York for a brief stint with the Yankees, to Pittsburgh, then back to Detroit to finish out the string; and, well . . . *me.*

(*The circle of life*—it moves us all.)

George Foster would later claim to reporters that his release was racially motivated, citing the call-up of a decidedly white Lee Mazzilli to support his claim, but when it was pointed out to him that Kevin Mitchell was his *true* replacement as the starting, slugging left fielder, and that Kevin Mitchell was just as black as he was, George Foster turned his attention to latching on with another team and jump-starting his career.

So here was Kevin Mitchell, a defensive jack-of-all-positions who was somehow not known for his defense, turning in a sparkling play that wiped the bases clean, lit up the crowd, and kept me on the mound for the time being. Really, that throw from left was such a crowd-pleaser, such an unexpected turn—especially when set against the dispiriting turns of the first two innings—that Mets fans rose to their feet as if on cue. And my heart rose right with them.

Here on in, I started mixing up my pitches—something I should have done right out of the gate. (Maybe Davey Johnson had been right to tell me to use *all* the pitches in my arsenal—early and often.) I got Evans to pop up to Mookie Wilson in center on a 1-0 breaking ball, and Gedman to chop an 0-1 pitch to Keith Hernandez at first, and before you could blink I was out of the inning. Again, it wasn't exactly a clean sheet, but it felt for a moment like I had turned some sort of page. Out of the five pitches I threw that inning, four of them were breaking balls, and I realized this was how I should have been pitching all along.

It's like a lightbulb went off—all of a sudden, I could see.

My first thought as I returned to the dugout was that I was due to bat, and this in turn got me thinking what this might mean. From a pure pitching standpoint, it was probably too early for Davey Johnson to give me the hook, especially with the quick inning I'd just put up on the board. Offensively, there weren't too many scenarios that would push him to lift me for a pinch hitter. Rafael Santana was scheduled to lead off; if he got on, the baseball move would be to bunt him over to second, so I'd get to stay in the game; if he got a double, the play was to bunt him to third; a triple, the pitcher would stay in and try to push the ball to the right side; if Raffy didn't get on, with one out, down three runs, you hit the pitcher. About the only scenario that would get Davey to even think about pinch-hitting for me was if Raffy somehow hit a home run—something he'd done just once the entire season—so it didn't look like I was going anywhere anytime soon.

Turned out Raffy struck out swinging, so I got to hit. I tried to make the most of it—first-pitch swinging at a ball up in the strike zone and sending Dwight Evans to the warning track in right to make the catch. I really drove that sucker. Against any other pitcher in the National League, Evans would have been playing in, and I'd be standing on second with a double, but he was playing me like a hitter, so I kicked the dirt in frustration as I rounded the bag at first. Of course, the Boston scouts had seen me play not all that long ago. They knew I could hit. So it followed that our hardest hit ball of the game so far was run down fairly easily, and I now would have just a few moments to gather my thoughts, grab my glove, and head back to the mound.

The baseball move in *this* scenario—after a pitcher makes an out—is for the next batter to take a couple of pitches and give the pitcher some time to regroup. It's standard operating procedure—Baseball 101. But the fundamentals didn't always apply with Mookie, only here he at least took his time leaving the batter's box and digging in at the plate. He even stopped to have a brief chat with home plate umpire John Kibler— whatever he could do to kill a little more time that didn't require him to be all that patient at the plate. This time around, he actually took a couple of pitches, ran the count to 2-1 before sending Evans to just about the same spot on the warning track, where he made the catch for the third out of the inning.

Mookie had hit the hell out of the ball, though, and a part of me thought we would take that into the middle innings, swing with a little more conviction, knowing we could get to Bruce Hurst. First Keith, then me, and now Mookie . . . we'd gotten good wood on the ball, so perhaps there was a take-away here. Perhaps we would find a way to solve Hurst before too long.

And yet our guys weren't thinking any such thing. Why? Because baseball is essentially a results-driven game. If you score, you score; if you string together a bunch of hits, you string together a bunch of hits; but if you hit the ball hard and it still finds the other guy's glove, well, then you've just made another out. But *I* was thinking in this way, at least. *I* was thinking that if I could keep mixing my pitches, notch another bunch of quick outs, we could start to peck away at this three-run lead, so I started out the fourth inning with a swagger I hadn't quite earned.

Dave Henderson was leading off, and I opened with a breaking ball for a called strike. It was the first good breaking ball I'd thrown all night, and if you added it to the four out of five breaking balls I'd thrown the previous inning it should have signaled to the Red Sox that I was a completely different pitcher from the rattled young gun who'd started the game. This was a good and welcome thing; I was settling in. But then I went and plunked Henderson on the second pitch—a split-finger fastball that got away from me—and I was back on that up-and-down roller coaster I'd been riding all night long.

One pitch, and I went from settling in to unsettled.

Gary Carter came out to the mound to talk to me, but this was another one of those moments when there was nothing much to say. *Hey, Ronnie. Try not to hit the next guy, too, okay?* He was mostly stalling, giving Sid Fernandez a few extra throws in the bullpen, but there was a strategy piece to it, too. With a runner on first and the bottom of the order coming up, we needed to guard against the bunt. But Spike Owen lined out to Darryl Strawberry in right on the very next pitch, so we were looking at a carbon copy of the situation we'd faced in the top of the second: Henderson on first, one out, Bruce Hurst at the plate looking to sacrifice. As before, Keith Hernandez came to the hill to discuss tactics, and here we agreed that I would throw once to first to keep Henderson close, and then try to bust Hurst inside with a fastball. As before, Keith charged the plate as I went into my motion, while Ray Knight moved in from the third-base side. Somehow, Hurst got the bunt down, and this time Ray fielded the ball cleanly and fired down to Timmy Teufel covering first as Henderson crossed to second.

And this time, my work was done. With Wade Boggs coming up in the leadoff spot, Davey Johnson had seen enough, and when I think back on this pitching change now, all these years later, I keep hearing that line from the classic Stones song "Beast of Burden" from back in college:

You can put me out. On the street . . .
But put me out, put me out. Put me out of misery

You know how certain closers arrange to have certain songs played when they're called into the game? Years later, Mariano Rivera would famously blast that energy-tinged Metallica song "Enter Sandman" every time he entered a game to pump himself up, set the tone, and here I'm thinking I could have used this wistful Stones song as my exit music. It neatly summed up how I was feeling—like I needed to be put out of my misery.

Anyway, I hadn't realized it when I was in its middle, but as soon as Davey pulled the plug on this outing it felt to me like a great weight was being lifted from my shoulders. It was the weight of disappointment, the weight of great expectations unrealized, the weight of letting down my teammates, my family, my city . . . Was I miserable? I didn't think so at the time. I was struggling, certainly. I was frustrated, disappointed. I was *done*. But I don't think I was truly miserable until I started that long walk back to the dugout.

Let's be clear: it was the right baseball move. Davey knew we couldn't afford to give up any more runs. He knew we were up against it. He knew Sid was ready. He wanted that lefty-lefty matchup with Boggs coming to the plate. But it rankled. Even though it made all kinds of sense, it rankled. I was too much of a competitor to see it from the manager's perspective, too young and green to take the long view. My arm felt good. I was starting to think I could turn the game around. But this was just the sweet admixture of bluster and bravado, with a dash of false hope. Inside, I was dying. And as soon as Davey pulled the plug I began to power down. As a professional, you work really hard on your body language; you're careful not to give anything away in terms of your emotions, your approach; good or bad, you're supposed to carry yourself the same way. So that's what I was all about here. I'd allowed myself a deep, deep breath after hitting Henderson—because, hey, I was frustrated. Pissed at myself and frustrated. And the thing of it is, I've spent these past pages knocking my effort, and the knocks are deserved, but I don't want to fail to acknowledge the role the Red Sox played in my dismal showing.

Realize, this was a veteran team that was facing me for the third time in ten days; obviously, they made better adjustments than I did. In the first two games, I probably got them out on a lot of balls down in the strike zone, a lot of fastballs, and I stupidly, haughtily assumed I could do the same in this Game 7. They made me pay, and as Davey gave the signal for the left-hander on his way out to the mound to take me from my dreams I allowed myself the slightest, most imperceptible smile. Why? Because I caught myself thinking of the sweet, unlikely connection that bound me to Sid Fernandez—thinking that this would be the first and last time you'd ever see a native-born Hawaiian pitcher replaced by another native-born Hawaiian pitcher in Game 7 of a World Series.

So there was *that*....

People ask me all the time what a manager says to a pitcher in this type of situation. Usually, it's just a string of baseball clichés. *Way to go, big guy. You'll get 'em next time.* There's a pat on the ass, a clap on the back ... whatever. It's less about what's said in the moment than it is about the moment itself. Davey wasn't much for imparting any great words of wisdom when he went out there to take a pitcher out of the game. What was there to say, really? Then as now, the counseling sessions were left to the pitching coach, who'd be sent out to calm a pitcher down or talk strategy. The manager was the guy who asked for the ball—that's it. And it's not like Davey Johnson would sidle up to you in the dugout after your day was through and talk through how the game might have gone differently, what he'd like to see more of next time out. No, once you were done, you were done—in *Godfather* terms, I was dead to him.

The long walk back to the dugout was dreadful on top of dreadful. I was embarrassed—too ashamed to look up at the crowd. I've talked about this before, but in all of team sports there's nothing quite like the walk of shame that finds a pitcher being chased from a game due to his own piss-poor performance. You're called out for all the world to see. But there was no chorus of boos, which would have been deserved. That's why I'll always love our fans. They knew I was hurting. There was no need to pile on. There was even a smattering of polite applause, as if to say, *No worries, big guy. You'll get 'em next time.*

Such an agonizing moment! It was sickening, really, and here I do mean *really*. I was actually sick to my stomach, like the time I lost sight of my parents at the beach when I was a kid, and in the minute or so it took me to find them my stomach dropped and I felt this sad, desperate ache. That's what this was like, only more so. I was tired, too—like, *bone* tired. I hadn't realized this, either, but as soon as I was pulled my body shut down. Maybe it was the pressure catching up to me. Maybe it was the fact that I hadn't slept very well the past couple of days. Maybe it was the rainout, causing me to double-down on the tension. Whatever it was, I was completely drained, and it wasn't until years later when I read an interview with Tiger Woods where he said that every time he'd win a Major he'd go home and be unable to get out of bed for a week, with flu-like symptoms, that I thought, *Hmmm . . .*

that's what used to happen to me. Big games, big moments . . . they were almost always followed by a period of time when I felt spent, weary, and here it hit me before I got to the dugout. It was all I could do to sit myself down and hold my head high and hope like crazy Sid Fernandez could clean up my mess so we could get back in the game.

MIDDLE INNINGS

Just like that, I was done. Wasn't exactly how I'd written this moment in my head. Wasn't how I'd imagined it, going back nearly twenty years to October 1967 when I could close my eyes and pretend I was taking the hill for my beloved Red Sox for Game 7 of the World Series against the St. Louis Cardinals. Not even close.

But I wasn't done just yet. I was still responsible for Dave Henderson on second. There was nothing I could actually *do* about him, but that's one of the funny expressions that attaches to the game. I'd put him on base, so if he came around to score it would be on me.

Of course, it would be on Sid Fernandez, too. He wasn't conditioned to think like a relief pitcher, but he felt the same responsibility. All relievers think in this way when they enter a game with runners on base. They want to put out the fire, erase the threat. That's their role. Sid was new to this type of pitching, but he was a fiery competitor. (Okay, so maybe "fiery" isn't the best word to describe my Hawaiian brother, since he had a chill, laid-back island persona, but he hated to lose, was quick to adapt to whatever the game threw at him, so I'll go with it anyway.) He'd already made two relief appearances in this series—in Game 2, when he started the ninth inning on the short end of a one-sided 8–3 score; and in Game 5, in relief of Doc Gooden, when he came on in the fifth with runners on first and third, no outs. In Game 2, he gave up back-to-back singles to start the inning, eventually leading to a tack-on run; in Game 5, down 3–0 on the scoreboard, as he was here, he struck out Rich Gedman on three pitches before giving up a double to Dave Henderson, scoring the inherited runner at third.

For the record, Sid went on to retire the next nine batters, and closed out Game 5 without allowing another run—that's how dominant he could be once he dialed in, and I don't think there was anyone in the ballpark pulling for him harder than me to be just as dominant this time out. Why? Because I felt *responsible* for Sid, too. I'd put him in this tough spot, so until he could pitch his way out of it, it was on me.

Those big-game jitters that seemed to be contagious back in the first inning? Sid caught a slight case of his own before finding his way. He walked Boggs on six pitches, although in this particular tough spot that wasn't such a terrible outcome. First base was open, and Sid had to be careful not to give the guy anything good to hit. Even so, he looked a little wild, a little tentative; he was out to hit the corners, but he missed wide on a couple of pitches, left me thinking he was overthrowing, being super-tentative.

The thing about Sid, he didn't look like any other pitcher

in baseball. He was a good athlete, but he didn't have the body of an athlete. He had a low release point—it almost looked as though he was throwing uphill. He probably clocked in at about five miles per hour slower than me, best fastball to best fastball, but the margin was lost in his unorthodox motion. He came at you from an entirely different angle.

His assignment was clear: throw as hard as you can for as long as you can. He wasn't tasked to think like a starter in this situation. It was the last game of the season. Every pitcher on our staff was available—save perhaps for Bobby Ojeda, who'd gone six innings two nights before and was therefore only available *in extremis*. We didn't need six or seven innings out of Sid. We just needed him to get us out of this one—and maybe the one after that, and the one after that. If he faltered, or tired, Davey could have looked to Doc Gooden, who'd started Game 5 four nights earlier, or to Rick Aguilera, or to our experienced relief corps. There was no room for a misstep at this point— I'd already taken all the missteps we were allowed as a team if we still hoped to win this thing, so I guess I was responsible for *that*, too.

This seems as good a spot as any to reflect on Doc's role on that 1986 team, since he loomed as an option now that I'd let the game get away from us. I might have gotten the spot on that *Sports Illustrated* cover, to represent our "pitching-rich Mets," but Doc was our number-one starter, no question. You put together a guitar army in a group like the Yardbirds, somebody's got to step up and be Eric Clapton, right? And yet even Doc would probably tell you the designation had more to do with his reputation than his performance on the field that year. We all pitched in his shadow, but even Doc was pitching in his own shadow at that point in his career. And you have to realize, a phrase like that—*at that point in his career*—shouldn't even apply in this case, because Doc was just twenty-one years old. Naively, I thought he was simply adjusting to the changes to his body. Years later, Doc would talk bravely and openly about his drug use, but at the time I was blind to that sort of thing. I really did think it was physical—the changes in his game, in his approach, in his effectiveness. I mean, he was still growing when he joined the team, at nineteen years old, and he went from being this rail-thin whippersnapper at 6'1", 6'2", maybe 190 pounds, to a more imposing 6'4", maybe 220 pounds, so it made sense that he was playing catch-up, trying to find a way to get that whippersnapper torque on his fastball with his new frame.

Doc's 1985 season was one of the greatest campaigns ever for a pitcher. He was just so damn dominant, so much fun to watch, that when his performance fell off a little bit in 1986 we all scratched our heads and wondered what the hell was going on. People used to ask me all the time, "What's wrong with Dwight?" And I'd tell them his body was changing and he was going to have to figure that out. I'd tell them it was an adjustment, and I guess it was, only not for the reasons I thought at the time.

Still, Doc was our go-to guy at the top of our rotation, even if he was getting by on reputation and fumes. He wasn't anywhere close to the pitcher he'd been his first two seasons, but those seasons were so trail-blazingly brilliant it's like he'd been placed on a special pedestal—a spot he continues to occupy in the minds of many Mets fans. In the space of a season, he went from immortal to merely mortal . . . and, somehow, it was enough to get him to seventeen wins.

He was like our Eddie Murphy, the way I look at it. Remember when Eddie first joined the cast of *Saturday Night Live*? Nobody had ever seen anything like him When he took the stage, it's like he was lit from within. For a few trailblazingly brilliant years, the show seemed to revolve around him. He made a couple of blockbuster movies during this period, and he was at the heart of those, too. Everyone stopped what they were doing to watch this kid do his thing—and then, after a couple of years, whatever *edge* he'd had was smoothed over. Soon, it was impossible to distinguish his fine body of work from the work of the other performers on the show, on the set. Either they'd caught up to him, or he started to relax a little bit, maybe rest on his laurels, and he slipped in with the rest of the pack.

And yet that trail-blazing brilliance was enough to light Eddie Murphy's reputation for all time—same way it did for Doc. People talk about them both in reverential tones, but the reverence is for a flashpoint, a moment in time that didn't last nearly as long as it should have, as it might have. And here Doc's standing on our depth chart was something Davey Johnson had to consider. In a lot of ways, going with Doc would have been a bulletproof move for Davey to make—a move nobody could have second-guessed. Maybe Doc wouldn't have tanked to start the game. Maybe he should have gotten the ball instead of me. Maybe he should have come on in relief instead of Sid. Maybe he should be the next arm out of the bullpen if Sid ran out of gas or if Davey had to lift him for a pinch hitter.

Maybe, maybe, maybe . . . and underneath all those *maybes* there was the specter of Doc's brilliant 1985 season, his breathtaking rookie season in 1984, and the melancholy thought that he could somehow tap into some of that same magic and put it to work for us yet again.

But Davey Johnson didn't have the luxury of thinking in hypotheticals. This was a *real* mess we were now facing, thanks to yours truly—not a hypothetical mess. Davey was just thinking outs. He could only manage by how Sid pitched, so these next batters were an important barometer; if Sid was *on*, Davey would keep him out there; if he was *off*, he'd be back in the dugout with me. Trouble was, the space between *on* and *off* can be difficult to distinguish until you start to work your way through the lineup. It's not like there's a switch you can flip and tell immediately what kind of outing you'll have. A lot of times, it takes a pitcher awhile to find his rhythm, especially if he's used to starting, especially if he's coming into the game in the middle of an inning with runners on base, and here it looked like Sid was still finding his way with Marty Barrett. First couple of pitches, he was a little too careful with the hot-hitting second baseman, but he was able to wheedle him into hitting a soft liner to Darryl Strawberry in right for the final out of the inning.

Okay, so *now* I was done. Now I was no longer responsible for anything that happened on the field—not directly, anyway. Now I could tell my brain to stop whirring through all these different scenarios. The funny baseball expression that attaches to this condition is that the book had been closed on my performance, which naturally leads me to wonder what the hell I'm doing opening it up and revisiting those wounds in these pages. Truth be told, it would be years before I stopped obsessing about those two "mistake" pitches I'd thrown to Evans and Gedman, about how predictable I'd been with my game plan—and just then I had no way to know if I'd ever again get to step on such a grand stage. Just then I had no idea this game would follow me around like a storm cloud. At the time all I could think was that I'd been in this big spot and failed to deliver. The stuff of my boyhood dreams—of *every* boyhood dream—had slipped through my split-fingers. It was a disappointment that would morph into regret over time, a regret that was only somewhat softened by the fact that we came back to win the game, the World Series, the whole damn deal. But it was a regret just the same—and the victory that came on the back of it left me feeling like we'd won the game *in spite of me* and not *because of me*.

The difference was everything.

Here's my pitching line again, just to attach some raw numbers to my piss-poor performance:

IP	H	R	ER	BB	K
3.2	6	3	3	1	0

Now, I don't mean to beat myself up in these pages, but there's no way to overstate how down I was as my teammates took the field for the top of the fifth inning. I caught myself wishing I was more religious, so I could pray for runs, beg for forgiveness, repent . . . *something*. I went to the clubhouse to take off my jersey, un-tape my ankles, put some distance between myself and the moment. That walk of shame, from the mound to the dugout after I'd been pulled from the game? There was a companion piece to it, and it was tucked away from public view. It came on the familiar path from the dugout to the clubhouse—up the steps, across the frayed Astroturf, down another short flight of stairs and into a clubhouse so eerily quiet it was like stepping into a cave.

Looking back, I can't think which was worse, which was longer—the walk from the mound or the walk from the dugout. On balance, I guess it always depended on how I'd pitched, the circumstances of the game. Here I'd pitched like shit, and the circumstances were lousy, so I'd have to say both walks were endlessly excruciating, but on this walk through the bowels of Shea Stadium I had a weird, almost out-of-body moment. You know how people who've had these near-death experiences talk about being called to the light? How the whole of their lives seems to flash in front of them? Well, it was a little like that for me here. I'd walked this path a hundred times, after good outings and bad, but never was it laced with so much meaning, so many layers of memory—never before, never since. As I walked, it felt to me like I was being pulled toward something—not a *light* necessarily, but a safe place. Like I was being lifted from a giant negative and being set back down in a kind of neutral zone.

As I walked, I could almost close my eyes and see the whole of my *baseball* life unfolding for me. There I was, in my Little League uniform, in my high school uniform, at Yale, at my first spring training with the Texas Rangers. There I was, facing Joe Morgan, Pete Rose, and Mike Schmidt in my first major league start—three future Hall of Famers, giving Rose his due, back-to-back-to-back . . . my own personal Murderer's Row. There I was throwing my first shutout in the bigs. There

I was at the All-Star game. There I was, *there I was* . . . and, now, here I was as well. Down and out and desperate for a way to set things right.

Of course, the *setting things right* would fall to my teammates, but there was a part of me that knew they would find a way to get it done. Just then, I could only kick myself. After a strong outing, walking from the dugout to the clubhouse, up and down those steps, my brain was always firing. I couldn't add two plus two, that's how locked in I was in those moments. But after a bad outing, after I'd been cuffed around, it was just the opposite. Everything was clear. I could add, I could subtract, I could ponder. I always thought it should have been the other way around—my brain should have been scrambled after a tough start. But instead I was able to get down on myself, to think of all the things I could have done differently, all the ways I could have stunk the place up just a little less.

I've known a lot of pitchers over the years who slog through a difficult outing and start to think their career is over. If they've been wild in just one outing, they worry they'll come down with a case of the yips. If there was no movement on their fastball, they worry it'll be flat here on in. They leave the game thinking they're *done*. But I never beat myself up in just this way. I was smart enough to know that horseshit was horseshit, and that natural ability was natural ability, and that once in a while the two switch places. That's why, every here and there, a horseshit pitcher throws a gem and an ace gets hit hard.

So here I was, stuck in clear mode, and there was no escaping the mess I'd made for my teammates. I felt sure it would be with me for all time. But it would not keep me from taking that hill yet again. It would not knock me from my spot in the rotation going into spring training. It would not keep me from dominating yet again—just as it would not keep me from getting hit hard yet again. It would be something to carry, that's all. Still, I needed these next few moments alone, and the clubhouse was empty, so I grabbed a pair of scissors and started cutting the tape from my ankles, tried to get lost in the mundane acts of ballplayer maintenance. It was a good distraction. I took off my jersey, my undershirt, my athletic tape, found a clean T-shirt and put it on in its place. There was no time to shower if I wanted to get back to the dugout to support my teammates—no reason to shower, come to think of it—but I wanted to be in dry clothes. I threw my warm-up jacket on over my shirt. Then, redressed, I sat on a chair in front of my locker for what felt like the longest time. It was just a half inning, but to me it was like all the time in the world.

Usually, there's nothing like the monotonous routine of a big-league clubhouse to take you out of your head for a bit, but here there was no escaping the mess I'd left out on that field. The familiar voice of radio play-by-play man Bob Murphy—one of the original "voices" of the New York Mets—was being piped in on the sound system, so the game was in my ears. I heard Murph make the call as Timmy Teufel struck out swinging, and thought what that might mean. I heard Murph get all excited as Keith Hernandez drove the ball hard to right-center, heard the rush of the crowd at the crack of the bat, *felt* the soft fall of disappointment when Dwight Evans was able to run the ball down . . . and thought what *that* might mean.

What it meant, taken together, was this: with each batter,

we were giving away precious outs. We were approaching the game's halfway mark—the point in the game where you start to think in a sand-through-the-hourglass sort of way. The second time through the lineup, you begin to see what adjustments you're able to make, what adjustments the opposing pitcher is able to make; a storyline for the game emerges, a likely outcome takes shape, and here it was starting to look more and more like this one was going against us. More and more, that was becoming the mood of the room—down here in the clubhouse, up there in the stands. Out there in the dugout, though, I had to think the mood told a different story. I had to think our guys were up, confident, all those good things, even though we couldn't get anything going.

For the time being, Hurst had us figured. Even when we hit him hard, we hit it right at someone. Every batter he set down was like another drag on my score sheet, and whatever bluster my teammates might have been feeling in the dugout was lost to me here in the clubhouse.

Here in the clubhouse, there was nothing to do but bitch and fume and tremble. If I could have kicked myself, I would have.

If I could have thrown a stool or knocked over a towel rack, I would have.

If I could have screamed without alerting a clubhouse attendant or security guard, I would have.

If I could have put my hand through the wall, I would have done that, too.

As I powered down, I thought for the first time about the death threat that greeted me as I arrived at the ballpark that afternoon. I'd put it out of my mind, completely out of my mind, but now that the adrenaline rush of the big game had coursed through my system, the reality of that threat realighted in my thinking. How crazy was *that*? I never knew if there was any merit or substance to it. I never knew what measures the police and security crew put in place to protect me. I only knew that it couldn't touch me, that threat, so I set it aside. But now that my big moment had passed in such a disappointing, dispiriting way, I thought again of that threat, wondered who would want to kill me, and why, and as soon as I framed the question in my head I allowed myself another small, slight smile—my second since Dwight Evans took me deep to start the second inning.

This time, I smiled because I realized I'd just blown the case wide open, and not in a good way. What was so damn funny to me, at just that moment, was the thought that I'd just given the police 50,032 new suspects to consider, because every Mets fan who'd come out to the park that night, every Mets fan who'd been waiting so patiently, so painstakingly for another World Championship now had sufficient motive to rub me out.

After all, it wasn't just *my* dreams that I'd dashed with my lousy start . . . it was theirs as well.

And, so, I laughed—and in that laugh was the bottled-up emotion of the past forty-eight hours, the tension of the long season. It all came bubbling forth, and it was a bracing release, and if anyone happened into the clubhouse at just this moment, if there had been security cameras in place to capture this scene for posterity, I would have looked just as crazy as the nut who'd issued the death threat in the first place. No, I wasn't laughing in a maniacal way, like I was hatching some diabolical plan; probably, I was just chuckling to myself at the absurdity of this one thought—but what was so absurd about it, really, was that these Mets fans hadn't sent me off with any bitterness or rancor. There were no boos that I could make out. No one seemed to want to string me up or run me out of town.

This alone was no reason to laugh, of course, but at the very least it was a reason to smile.

Carter was next, and he grounded weakly to second to end the inning, and for whatever reason I put a lot into this at bat— alone with my thoughts, slipping out of my battle armor, setting my game face aside. As I listened to Murph make the call I caught myself thinking what Kid meant to our team. That's another thing Mets fans seem inclined to forget—the significance of the trade that brought the future Hall of Famer to New York. You don't see too many trades like that anymore, with the entrenchment of free agency, but all these years later it's clear that Kid was the missing piece to our championship puzzle. To our general manager, Frank Cashen, this was clear at the time, which was why he went after Carter hard. Cashen used to tell reporters it was the most difficult deal he made in his entire career—not because it was tough to pull the trigger or because he had to part with too much talent or because he worried he'd be second-guessed by the fans and the media, but because Cashen's counterpart in Montreal, John McHale, was so reluctant to give up his franchise player.

Gary Carter was probably the closest thing to baseball royalty they'd ever seen in Canada, and McHale must have thought he'd be run out of the country for trading him away.

But Frank Cashen was persistent; he knew the Expos organization was eager to get out from under Carter's long-term contract, so he kept pressing, ultimately giving up Hubie Brooks, Mike Fitzgerald, Floyd Youmans, and Herm Winningham in December 1984. It was an all-in type moment for the Mets. We'd traded for the best first baseman in the game the year before, in Keith Hernandez; we'd had our first full season with the most exciting young player in the game, in Darryl Strawberry; and we'd just witnessed one of the most sparkling debut seasons by a rookie pitcher in a generation, in Dwight Gooden.

We needed a big bat, and an experienced catcher to handle our young pitching staff and drive our team to the next level, and we needed these things right away.

The feeling in the front office was that Gary Carter fit the bill on both fronts. And he did—absolutely, he did—only it took some of us players awhile to acknowledge this. You see, Gary Carter came with a reputation. His Montreal teammates called him Camera Carter—not the most flattering nickname, but he was a bit of a showboat. If he was still alive to defend himself, I don't think Gary would even bother to argue this point. He *loved* the spotlight. As a catcher, as a cleanup hitter, he appeared to relish in the way the game ran through him. And I think he knew full well that his teammates didn't always like him; even his opponents didn't care for him all that much. Me, I used to hate playing against him. You play against some guys and you come away thinking, *Boy, he's a gamer*, or, *Boy, I wish he was on my team*. But that was never the case with Kid. Not that he *wasn't* a gamer; it's just that his tenacity, his competitiveness, his drive—these weren't the first things you noticed about him on the other side of the diamond. No, you noticed that he was a little flashy, a little too much front and center—like I said, in the spotlight. That was his reputation, and it preceded him in New York in such a way that it colored our first impressions of him as a teammate.

When he joined our club, I tended to think of Kid as a holier-than-thou personality, but then I got to know him, understand him, appreciate him. I grew to love him—a lot of us did, even though there was a lot of head-butting that first season. Here in 1986, we were past that head-butting phase, the two of us, but we were not yet close. That would come later. By 1988, we were rock solid, but it took awhile. Looking back, though, I think we were all a little too quick to judge Kid on these aspects of his personality. After all, you don't get to be a major league ballplayer without being a hard-charger. You've got to have a little fight in you, right? You can't carry a team, a franchise, a city on your back unless you're willing to take the lead on the heavy lifting.

Still, he'd been the best catcher in the game for a decade, so most of us were happy to have him—and, over time, I was happy to have him calling games for me behind the plate. He made me a better pitcher. He understood the hitters. He was a special talent, but it took awhile for the two of us to truly connect, and these World Series games fell somewhere in the middle of that *while*. We were still clashing a bit on how to pitch certain hitters. And the thing of it is, Kid knew what he was doing, while I only *thought* I knew what I was doing. If I'd let him take the lead on my Game 7 approach, I might have still been out there, doing my thing.

Over time, I grew to trust him wholeheartedly. And

admire him, also wholeheartedly—especially for the way he played in pain. Catchers get dinged up a lot, and Gary Carter was no exception. But he was a veteran catcher working with a corps of some of the best young pitchers in the game, so he never felt like he could take a day off.

Realize, when I refer to our talented young pitching staff in this way, I'm not just crowing or blowing smoke. Four of our starters would finish in the top seven in the 1986 National League Cy Young Award balloting—Bob Ojeda was fourth; I was tied for fifth (with Pittsburgh's Rick Rhoden); and Dwight Gooden and Sid Fernandez were tied for seventh.

(For once, the "curse" of *Sports Illustrated*—the sports shibboleth that suggests that athletes featured on the cover are headed for a fall—didn't come to pass. Or, at least, it hadn't come to pass just yet, because after that "Armed Force" feature in August, we'd merely continued on in our lights-out way— although I guess in this moment the curse was still hovering over our season like a dark cloud, where it would remain until we could start putting some runs on the board.)

Anyway, that's a top-heavy Cy Young ballot we're not likely to see again in our baseball lifetimes, and Kid was a big reason for that. He had a tremendous feel for the game, and it sometimes seemed he knew more about the opposing hitters than they knew about themselves, so once I started to trust him I was able to grow my game. It got to where we even had our own secret handshake. (That's the kind of thing ballplayers do, so don't go thinking we were weird or uncool.) We both had big hands, so we came up with this handshake, and for years we'd greet each other in this big-handed way and enjoy this strong connection. (Okay, so this handshake business *does* sound a little weird and uncool in the retelling, but there it is.) In fact, one of my favorite pictures from my playing days is a shot of me from the 1988 season, on the day we beat the Phillies to clinch the NL East title. It's a shot of me and Kid shaking hands in our trademark way, flashing each other a kind of knowing, self-satisfied look that said, *Hey, we did it*, a look that said, *Hey, we're in this together.*

I don't keep a lot of pictures of me in uniform, but I've got this one framed, and every time I look at it, especially now with Kid gone, it takes me back to the enduring bond that can form between a pitcher and his catcher.

So there was Kid, coming over before the 1985 season with all this baggage, and it took awhile for a lot of the guys to fully embrace him. There were players on the Expos like Tim Raines and Andre Dawson who used to grouse that Gary got all the commercials and endorsement deals because he went out and learned how to speak French, but that's just the kind of thing you can easily take the wrong way. At first you might think Kid was trying to ace out his teammates, keep the shine to his image, but once you got to know him you saw he was going out of his way to connect with the Montreal fans and that the endorsements were just a by-product of that.

That bunt attempt he'd made, leading off the second inning? That one at bat offered the perfect example of how some people were quick to dismiss Kid as a showboat, out for himself. We talked about that play a lot on the bench, in the clubhouse, and on and on, and opinion was divided pretty much along party lines. Remember, we were down 3–0 at that point, and the entire stadium expected our cleanup hitter to come out swinging. Certainly, *I* expected Kid to come out swinging—and for all I know, Davey Johnson expected the same. But Kid tried to catch the Red Sox napping and leg out a bunt—not the most conventional move, as any baseball purist could tell you. But if you loved Gary, if you appreciated his baseball acumen, his grit, his desire, you saw it as a team leader thinking outside the box, trying to shake things up, get something going, *zigging* when his opponents were looking for him to *zag*. If you hated him, you could point to a play like that as selfish, mulish, maybe even a little big-headed. But that was just Gary hustling, scraping, doing whatever he thought needed doing to get his team back in the game.

Without even realizing it, without even giving it voice, I think we all came to rely on his experience, his professionalism, his poise, which was why I stood and listened as Bob Murphy described Carter's at bat for the radio listeners. A part of me believed the game would turn on this one at bat and that Kid would find a way to once again put the team on his back and propel us forward—to save my ass!—so when all he managed off Hurst was a six-hopper to Marty Barrett to end the inning, I could only sigh and think that if Kid couldn't turn this game around we were well and truly fucked.

For all the angst and anguish of those long, doleful walks from the mound and from the dugout, the time alone in the clubhouse can be lonelier still—it's like you've been sent to Siberia. Your teammates are out on the field, trying to clean up after you, while you're stuck in the solitary confines of an empty clubhouse, left to marinate in your misery.

For me, throughout my career, these long, low moments in the clubhouse after a disappointing start were always difficult—draining, dispiriting. They found me frequently enough that I fell into my own routine, but here on this night the routine didn't apply. It was the last game of the season. There was no reason to ice, no reason to ride the bike, no reason to work the stretch bands. I was completely done. There was nothing left but to think through the game, question every pitch, wonder how it was that I'd let the moment get away from me so quickly, so completely. There was time enough, even, to doubt the whole of my career.

You beat yourself up in these down moments. Anyway, I always did. Once, after a particularly lousy start in Cincinnati, I rode the stationary bike furiously as a kind of penance. This alone wasn't so unusual, but on this one night—July 19, 1988—I didn't even make it out of the first inning. The Reds were just all over me, and I was just nowhere: two-thirds of an inning, five hits, three walks, nine runs, five of them earned. I gave up back-to-back home runs to Chris Sabo and Eric Davis, and by the time Cincinnati had batted around and reached once again to Sabo's spot in the three hole, Davey Johnson had seen enough. I left the game with the bases loaded and the small, certain fear that I would never again pitch my way through an inning with nothing across. And so I hopped on that bike and rode it all the way through to the end of the game— two and a half hours of atonement for another lousy job.

Typically, though, I went through my motions, beat myself up just enough, and made my way back to the dugout. For the most part, the only times I'd remain in the clubhouse were if I'd gone seven or eight innings, and I still had my work to do, dialing down from the game. But other than that one dismal night in Cincinnati, and perhaps another time or two that I'm conveniently blocking from memory, I'd put myself through my postgame paces and rejoin my teammates. The bigger I was beat, the more important I thought it was to get back out there, because I had to own it. I had to take the hit—let it be known that *I* was the reason we were getting killed, and that I knew this as well as anyone. Ballplayers notice this kind of thing, they do. The guy who mopes around, all hangdog, all *woe is me* . . . he turns inward, and as he turns inward his teammates turn away. It spills over into how things are even when things are going well. If you put it out there that you don't really care how the game goes after your bad start, you also put it out there that you've made the game about *you.* You've set it up so you're set apart, when what you really want is to be in the mix along with everyone else, getting tossed around by the same swirl of emotions that can find you late in the game. What you really want is to will your teammates back into it, to lift them past these great new hurdles you've set out for them, to make like those crooked numbers you've allowed your opponents to put up on the scoreboard will somehow fall away.

The bigger the moment you've let slip from your grasp, the greater the need to choke down your pride, toughen your skin, and take your place on the bench, where the baseball gods might *still* find you and smile down upon you after all.

I went to the dugout for the top of the fifth and watched Sid work his way through the heart of the Red Sox order like nothing at all, and as I set up at the end of the bench I couldn't shake thinking I'd let my teammates down. It was a wearying thought. Nobody said anything to make me feel this way—in fact, I got a whole lot of claps on the back, a whole lot of re-assuring smacks of glove leather to my knees, and I collected these shows of support like I needed them to breathe.

Don't worry about it, Ronnie. We'll get those runs back.

Sid got Buckner to loft a lazy fly ball to Strawberry in right, then he came back to strike out Rice and Evans, each on three pitches—the first strikeouts of the game for our side. Those strikeouts had a galvanizing effect; they brought the crowd to its feet and lifted me from my doldrums, and as we careened past the game's halfway point it's like the fans were imploring the Mets to get something going.

Suddenly, we were all lit from within.

Inevitably, inexorably, that energy spilled over to our half of the inning. But energy alone wasn't going to give us base runners, and an interesting dynamic took shape between our long-suffering fans and the long-swaggering guys on our bench. The crowd would rise, my teammates would dig in and try to get a rally going, we'd hit the ball hard and nothing would come of it. We were up and down, up and down, riding which-ever wave seemed likely to take us where we needed so des-perately to go. My teammates, meanwhile, were still feeling cocky—to a man they would have told you we would find a way to "solve" Bruce Hurst before too long. And I might have agreed with them, only with each nail in our team coffin, with each notch in Hurst's belt, the momentum seemed to leak once again from that old stadium.

Strawberry flied out to center.

Knight chopped out to short.

Mitchell struck out swinging.

And just like that, we were up against it yet again. Still.

As before. The whoops and hollers that followed Sid's one-two-three inning in the top of the fifth were quieted, and in their place was the nagging sense that time was conspiring against us, and the mood of the room shifted back and forth in this way for the next while. It was a regular seesaw battle, only the two teams weren't trading any blows. The score wasn't changing; the complexion of the game wasn't changing so much as deepening. The only discernible change was how each side was feeling about its chances, and on our side we were up and down, back and forth, here and there with each shift.

And then, top of the sixth, Sid Fernandez went out and kick-started another momentum swing, striking out Gedman on three pitches for his third strikeout in a row. Once again, the crowd was into it. Once again, we reminded ourselves that we were supposed to feel invincible, and when Henderson hit a nothing fly ball to Mookie in left-center, and Spike Owen went down looking, the crowd was whipped into another frenzy.

And as the fans stood and cheered Sid as he left the field, I allowed myself a small, sweet, certain thought: if the crowd was coming alive, then the Mets wouldn't be far behind.

Bruce Hurst had retired ten batters in a row, reaching back to that Ray Knight single in the bottom of the second— our only hit of the game—and there was a feeling in the air that his luck had to change. That *our* luck was about to change.

Really, it had to.

9

GAME ON THE LINE

It was a little strange, trying to reposition myself among my teammates after that decompression time in the clubhouse—strange, that is, for me, because I realize now that the other guys on the bench probably didn't give my presence too much thought. Still, a part of me felt like some kind of interloper, like I belonged someplace else. To their great credit, to a man, my teammates took the time to acknowledge me as I sat down on the bench. I was on the receiving end of about a dozen "glove taps"—you know, the manly touch of leather to jersey that has been passed from teammate to teammate for generations. It's the ballplayers' version of *aloha*—it can mean just about anything:

Shake it off.

Hang in there.

Don't worry about it.

Only here I took the gesture to mean, *Thanks a lot, R.J. Nice hole you've dug for us here.*

Okay, okay . . . so this was just me projecting. This was just me imagining that everyone was cursing me under their breath for dooming our chances. And who knows, maybe they were, in that place deep down that athletes don't always like to talk about, think about. All I knew for certain was that it was an agonizing, wearying thing, to be made to consider that you'd let your teammates down—and to know that you've disappointed an entire city as well. And forget everybody else in the dugout, in that stadium, in that town . . . there was my own regret as well.

(Who am I kidding? There was my own regret *most of all*.)

It's been thirty years, and I can still taste the acrid frustration that hung beneath the low ceiling of that Shea Stadium dugout, bouncing off those old concrete walls and churning my stomach. It's a taste that clutches at my throat every time I see another athlete on the desperate, dispiriting end of a similarly low moment. I see myself in him . . . or *her*. As I write this, in July 2015, I'm watching the semifinal game in the Women's World Cup between England and Japan. It's the last minute of extra time in the second half, the score knotted at 1–1, the game headed to overtime, when an England defender lunges for the ball to clear it from the goal mouth and accidentally kicks it into her own goal. *Oh, my goodness . . .* Immediately, a million hearts break for this young woman—Laura Bassett, a respected veteran who'd played for the women's national team for over a dozen years. Another million break for dear old England—and then, a million more, just for the hell of it. Even supporters of Japan can't help but feel for this player (the Japanese players, too!), and as I take in the anguished look on her face as the clock ticks off the final few seconds and

Laura Bassett comes to realize the weight of this *own goal* she will now have to carry for the rest of her days, I am reminded yet again of the goat horns I carried with me from the clubhouse that night.

Alas, there is no comparing these low moments. Laura Bassett's miscue cost her team a trip to overtime, with no guarantees that they would have made it on to the finals. My collection of miscues cost my team a measure of momentum and juice, as we looked to get and keep an edge in this deciding game of a seven-game championship series. One, there is no recovering from; the other, there is still a fighting chance. And yet as I watch this young woman collect the hugs and commiserations and "glove taps" of her broken teammates, I can't shake thinking that Laura Bassett has just joined the mercifully short list of people who can tell you what I was feeling on that uncertain October night, all those years ago.

How much did it suck, just then, being me? Bill Buckner could have told you, out there on the field, a couple of steps behind first base. Fred Snodgrass, seventy-four years earlier, could have told you, after dropping a routine fly ball and putting the tying run on base in what was probably the best-known blunder in World Series history . . . that is, until our own Game 6 just two nights before. Laura Bassett, now, can do the same. Absolutely, the way I'd kicked it in this start of starts was the baseball equivalent of an *own goal,* but I could only shake it off, hang in there, get 'em next time . . . and, basically, look for ways to convince myself that I hadn't just put my team on life support. That the *fighting chance* I'd barely left us with was still within reach, and, relatedly, that there was *fight* enough in my still-battling teammates to see us through.

There were certain cheerleading aspects of the game that were unavailable to me that night going forward. If you remember, those Mets teams were the progenitors of the "rally cap" tradition you now see in ballparks all over the country. It started somewhere in the stands, sometime during the 1985 season. The Shea faithful would inside-out their official Mets caps (because, naturally, the special sorcery of the rally cap wouldn't work with any old baseball cap), put it on (forward or backward, it didn't much matter), and hope for the best. If you could work it out that you were chewing gum and skilled enough in this area to blow a bubble the size of your face, this was thought to be helpful. Sometimes, an experienced rally cap sorcerer would remove that full-blown bubble from his mouth and stick it to the knob or the brim of his turned-up cap, and this too was known to add to the cap's special powers. Also, it helped every once in a while to take off the hat, flip it over, and shake it in front of you like you were sifting flour, intoning the baseball spirits to please, please, please drop some runs from the night sky into the open lid. Baseball fans (and, baseball players, it turns out) are a superstitious bunch, so once these intonations seemed to work a time or two—or, at least, to coexist in a coincidental way with a positive development— we turned to them again and again. All during this postseason run, from that nail-biting league championship series against Houston to these excruciating late games against Boston, we had our rally caps out, hoping against hope the game might lean our way. And, usually, it did. It seemed to us Mets that we *always* found a way to rally. To this day, I'll meet people who tell me they were in the crowd at Shea on the night of Game 6, their hats on inside-out in prayer, and they're *still* convinced that they somehow helped to put a whammy on poor Bill Buckner as that ball trickled through his legs.

And, who knows . . . maybe they did.

Sure enough, the rally caps were out on this night, too, more and more fervently, desperately, as we approached these late innings. The flour-sifting, the bubble gum–working, the prayerful looks to the heavens—it was all on full display in our dugout and out in the bullpen, only for me to participate in these rituals would have been a little clownish, a little churlish. (More than a little, actually.) It was something for the other guys on the team, something for the fans . . . but not something for me. Not on this night. After the way I'd pitched, I could only call out to the baseball gods in silence.

I had to be mindful of my part in this play.

We'd hit Bruce Hurst hard in the last couple of innings, so as Rafael Santana took his spot in the batter's box to lead off the sixth I caught myself looking for some kind of tell on the mound, to see if maybe the left-hander was finally flagging. A lot of times, a pitcher will give himself away in a tough spot. Maybe he'll let out an extra-long sigh between pitches, or look into his dugout a few times too many. Maybe he'll start to work a little more quickly, or a little more slowly, depending. It can be like a high-stakes poker game, the way ballplayers are checking one another out, searching for a sign of weakness. What you're looking for, really, is anything beyond the ordinary choreography, a break in the routine. I've seen guys wipe their brow a bunch of times late in the game when they were starting to tire, when they hadn't wiped their brow even once before that. I've seen other guys study the inside of their gloves a beat too long, as if they held some state secret. Some pitchers take off their caps and press down their hair with their palms. Sid Fernandez used to pull up the sides of his pants when he was sagging—but, alas, it wasn't his pants that were sagging, it was him. Me, I used to scratch at the mound with my right toe, head down. All game long, I'd go about my business, but when I was scrambling I was all about kicking the dirt, like I was looking for answers, buried clues, when in reality all I was doing was buying time—and, giving myself away.

With Hurst, I couldn't see anything in his demeanor, anything in his delivery to signal that his tank was running low—and yet with each half inning we seemed to reel him in a little closer. It's like we were catching up to him, but Raffy wasn't a patient-enough hitter to wait Hurst out, give our guys time to get a better read on him, and here he slapped a nothing chopper to Spike Owen on a 1-1 pitch for the first out of the inning—an out we didn't have to spare.

Next up was Lee Mazzilli, pinch-hitting for Sid. Just seeing Mazzilli in the on-deck circle was enough to stir the crowd, put the kettle on simmer. Remember, Maz had pinch-hit for us in Game 6 and helped to jump-start our unlikely comeback, scoring the tying run, so the fans quite reasonably saw him as a kind of good luck charm. Plus, he was a huge fan favorite, going back to his first tour of duty with the team, when he was the closest thing the Mets had to a superstar, so the air was suddenly filled with a mess of warmth and good cheer—although, I suppose, this was also me projecting.

At this point, Hurst had retired eleven in a row, but he wasn't dominating. There was nothing intimidating about his approach—our guys were eager to step in against him and take their cuts, whereas when a pitcher is *firing* they might want to hang back, skip their turn in the batting order. Earlier in the series, sure, Hurst had been occasionally untouchable, but that wasn't the pitcher we were seeing in this Game 7. We'd been hitting him hard, and there was a feeling up and down our bench that the ball would eventually fall our way. Trouble was, with one out in the bottom of the sixth, we were running out of *eventually*.

But here it was . . . *here it was*.

Maz faked a bunt on the first pitch. Ball one.

The next pitch was high. Ball two.

In this spot, I could only assume that Mazzilli was taking, and he was—only the ball caught the outside corner for a strike.

Then he jumped on the next pitch and sent a sweet little flare down the right-field line, foul. Strike two.

And finally, with the count tangled at 2-2, Maz stroked a hard grounder in the hole between short and third, for a *no doubt about it* single.

It was a solid piece of hitting from a veteran player, working a veteran pitcher to advantage, and it sent Mets fans to their feet. That simmering kettle? We'd gone from a slow boil to a rolling boil, just on the back of this one at bat, and here was Mookie Wilson, stepping to the plate beneath the corresponding din, looking to turn up the heat a little more. He was first-pitch swinging—Mookie being Mookie—which worked out for us in this spot, because he stroked a soft line drive into short left field, in pretty much the exact spot as Mazzilli's single.

(I can't be sure, but baseball historians might someday suggest the same blades of outfield grass were involved in each play.)

Runners on first and second, one out—rally caps firmly in place. There was chanting, rhythmic clapping, all of that. One of the great things about Mets fans, about Shea Stadium, was the signature "Let's Go Mets!" cheer that seemed to spring up on its own, a cadenced cry of endless hope. It was simple, basic, unadorned . . . and here it was, issuing forth from these first signs of life. As Tim Teufel stepped in and the crowd began to whip itself into a small frenzy, we could all see that Hurst was on his heels. There was no *one* tell but, rather, a group of tells. Suddenly there was a whole lot less swagger to Hurst's demeanor. In the space of just a half-dozen pitches, he'd been figured out, and now, for the first time, there was activity in the Red Sox bullpen.

Now, for the first time, there was something doing.

Timmy was up there swinging, too. At least, he meant to be. Hurst missed the strike zone on his first two pitches, so Timmy held back, but now with the count 2-0 we all knew he'd be looking for a ball over the plate. It was a hitter's count, and Timmy had been hitting Hurst pretty well—he was 4-9 against him for the series—so the instinct here was to drive the ball, keep the pressure on. But Bruce Hurst was a professional pitcher who knew Timmy would come out a little jumpy after those back-to-back singles, the crowd going a little crazy. So he pulled the string on his next pitch, took a whole lot off it, and Timmy was all the way out in front and could only flail at it. Still, the crowd continued to roar.

Hurst followed with a sinker, low and inside—clearly,

hoping to get Teufel to offer at it, but Timmy laid off. Then, with the count at 3-1, the chanting got a little louder, a little more purposeful:

"Let's go Mets!"

"Let's go Mets!"

"Let's go Mets!"

It's like the stadium was suddenly lifted by song, like these three words were a part of us. They were on our lips like they belonged no place else; and there was nothing for Timmy to do but take the next pitch. It was the percentage play—and the pitch was low and inside, to load the bases.

Red Sox manager John McNamara moseyed to the mound at this point, just to calm the crowd and give Hurst a chance to settle, maybe talk about how they wanted to pitch to Keith Hernandez, who'd driven the ball hard his last couple of times up. There was no urgency to McNamara's gait as he made the trip, but there was urgency in the moment, because we were about to boil over.

Finally, a tell: I noticed Bruce Hurst tugging at his sleeves a bit more than usual. Keith, I'm sure, noticed the same, so he stepped out before Hurst could throw a pitch, get inside his head a little bit, give the moment time to get a little bigger. But the next pitch from Hurst belied the notion that the game was getting to him, because he came back with a perfect opening salvo—a big, slow curve ball that looped across the plate for a called strike. Keith was fairly frozen, had been thinking fastball, could only look on in admiration, frustration. But then Keith crushed an inside pitch toward the gap in left-center field, and when it dropped for a hit the crowd went crazier still. Maz and Mookie came around to score, Teufel crossed to third, and it felt to me like the weight I'd been carrying since Evans and Gedman had taken me deep to start the second inning was about to be lifted.

What was great about this moment was that Keith had hit the ball on the nose his first couple of times at the plate in this game with no result. And here he was jammed and somehow managed to drive the ball and get us on the scoreboard, so he was rewarded for those earlier at bats. Baseball can be funny that way. It has a knack for balancing the scales—over a long season, certainly; over a single game, occasionally—and here we needed just one more run to get those scales back to even.

This was my one thought just then, to get back to even. To get me off the hook. The thought of actually *winning* the game was still paramount, but I was prioritizing here. The one would follow from the other, so as the crowd went crazy I offered up a silent prayer: *give me one more run—please, please, please.*

Davey Johnson sent in Wally Backman to pinch-run for Teufel, who now represented the tying run, ninety feet from home plate. The move gave the crowd another reason to cheer—it put it out there that this was our moment, time to move in for the kill—and for the first time since I'd returned to the bench from the clubhouse I ventured onto the top step, closest to the field, to see what I could see.

Carter was first-pitch swinging, too—he could see Hurst was reeling, thought he'd be looking to get ahead in the count. Kid ended up swinging at a ball out of the strike zone, low, but he was able to fist it on a looping line to short right field. Dwight Evans, an exceptional fielder, an eight-time Gold Glove Award winner, charged at the crack of the bat, and for a moment it looked like he might have a play on it. Backman tagged at third, knowing he could probably score if Evans made the catch, but Keith was kind of hung up between first and second, waiting to see what happened.

What happened was Evans dove forward and *appeared* to make the catch, but as he hit the ground the ball came loose. It took an extra beat or two for right-field umpire Dale Ford to signal if Evans had made the catch, so as Backman trotted home with the tying run, Keith was frozen on the base path. Evans was able to right himself and throw the ball back into the infield to get the out at second base. It should have been a single, runners on first and second, the score tied at 3–3, but instead it went down as a fielder's choice—same result on the scoreboard, but a whole different complexion on the inning.

Anyway, my silent prayer was answered. We'd gotten one more run to tie the game and I was off the hook . . . at long last. (*Spit the bit*—that's the term us ballplayers used, especially us pitchers staring down a loss.) We were back to even, and in my head the game that wasn't *really* about me but should have probably been *a little bit more about me* was no longer about me at all.

Keith was pissed—he left the field jawing at home plate umpire John Kibler, but in looking at the replay all these years later it just looked like a bad break. Evans had smothered the ball in such a way that it wasn't entirely clear if he'd made the catch. Dale Ford made the call as soon as he could, and Keith was in a tough spot, that's all. Still, it was a tough spot we could all live with—me, especially. It wiped the slate clean on my performance, filled the hole I'd dug for us, put us back in the game. And, significantly, it took the "L" from my pitching line. As a starting pitcher, you never wanted to see that "L" alongside your name in the box score the next morning. Pitchers think about this sort of thing, they do. End of the day, end of a season, end of a career, your body of work is defined by the wins and losses on your stat line. Everybody always talked about how the "cheap" wins tended to cancel out the "tough" losses over time, but after each game we all wanted to stay out of the minus column. That's just human nature, right? Nobody wanted a "Larry"—that's what we all called it. Ideally, you wanted that "W"—or, "Willie," but short of that you'd take a "Nelson Doubleday," which was what we called a "No Decision," after the publishing magnate who bought the Mets a couple of years before I joined the team, the great, great-grandnephew of Abner Doubleday, the man once thought to have invented the game of baseball in a pasture just outside Cooperstown, New York.

And, here, a Nelson Doubleday was looking pretty damn good right about now.

(Sadly, Mr. Doubleday died of pneumonia as I was putting the finishing touches to these pages, at the age of eighty-one, and as I read his obituary I thought back to the way his great name became synonymous in our clubhouse with this one measure of our pitching performance—a stat that essentially meant you were neither here nor there, that you hadn't really played the game at all.)

The fans, they could live with this new state of affairs, too. Suddenly, it was a ball game. Where there was once wishful thinking there was now pandemonium, and it felt for a sweet moment like those miserable early innings had happened on some other night long ago, to some other collection of hopefuls.

Then, another tell: Hurst threw over to first a time or two before turning to face Darryl Strawberry. Carter was no threat to run—he even had his foot on the bag—but Hurst seemed to need to take these few moments to gather his thoughts, catch his breath, let the momentum out of the stadium before dialing back in.

Darryl was also feeling *hitterish,* looking to continue our volley of punches, and he went the other way with a first-pitch sinker, slicing a ball to left field that Jim Rice had to charge to collect. It looked for a moment like the ball would tail away from Rice and drop for a hit, but he ended up making a nice diving catch to end the inning, and as Darryl kicked the dirt around first and turned for our dugout I couldn't shake thinking that this game was now ours.

We'd only just managed to tie the score, but the game had now leaned our way.

One of the cardinal rules in baseball is to keep the other team off the board after you've scored a bunch of runs to turn a game around—the *shut-down inning,* it's called—so it fell to our sinker-baller Roger McDowell to keep the score where it was. This was his fifth appearance of the series, so these Red Sox hitters had some good looks at him by now, but Roger was a gamer. He didn't shrink from his chances. The guys had a lot of confidence in him as he stood on that hill, but it didn't get close to the confidence Roger had in himself.

John McNamara sent up Tony Armas to pinch-hit for Bruce Hurst, but this was hardly the intimidating turn it might have been. Armas was just two years removed from a monster 1984 season, in which he led the American League in home runs and runs batted in, but he was no longer the same player. He'd been battling leg injuries, had seen his playing time reduced—especially when Boston traded for Dave Henderson in the middle of the season. This was Armas's first at bat of the series, so he'd yet to get a good look at Roger—and, happily, Roger was able to strike him out on three pitches.

Next, Roger got Wade Boggs to chop an 0-2 pitch to Ray Knight at third—only here Ray made it a little interesting, sending an errant throw across the diamond that Keith Hernandez was able to dig out on a short hop. I don't think there was another first baseman in the game who could have scooped a ball like that so effortlessly, but we were all so used to Keith's prowess by this point we didn't think anything of it as he made the play. It takes watching the replay in slow motion to appreciate the enduring impact Keith had on this game, on both sides of the ball. He'd gotten the big hit in the bottom of the sixth to set the stadium rocking, and here he made this sweet pick in the top of the seventh to keep the energy on our side, but he did it so efficiently, so gracefully it was easy not to notice.

Marty Barrett grounded out to Raffy at shortstop on the very next pitch, and just like that the bat was back in our hands.

This is as good a spot as any to reflect on the many gifts of my friend and uniquely talented teammate Keith Hernandez—Mex, to his teammates. Just so you know, no one else in baseball would have made this play—at least, not with any regularity or certainty. But Keith was cut a whole different way from other first basemen of his generation. He was separate and apart, above and beyond. He was, hands down, the single best all-around player I ever played with or against. He wasn't especially fast, but there was a quickness about him, a fluidity in the way he covered all that ground around first base that made his movements appear almost balletic. He had such perfect control of his body that when he dove for a ball he'd not only make the play but he'd be in a position to spring back to his feet and be ready to throw, or charge toward second, or perform whatever follow-up movement was required.

He was just one of those guys you knew would find a way to execute. Big plays always seemed to find his glove—and, more than that, he changed the way the game was played. He was the most aggressive defensive player I've ever seen, in all my years in the game. And the most focused. He was completely on point, from the first pitch to the final out of the game; I never once saw his intensity level drop, not for one moment. And he was clutch. I know there's a tendency these days to look at the analytics and announce that there's no such thing as a "clutch" ballplayer—that the numbers tell you an athlete performs a certain way over time, with little variation in that performance owing to key game situations. But those numbers didn't apply with Mex. He was clutch, no doubt about it. With the game on the line, there was no one you'd rather see up at the plate, no one you'd rather see on the receiving end of an errant throw. Here in these back-to-back frames, the bottom of the sixth and the top of the seventh, the baseball world had a chance to see him stand and deliver, while those of us who played with him every day knew full well he would do just that.

When Keith joined the Mets in that midseason trade with the St. Louis Cardinals in 1983, he changed the culture of our entire organization. I was called up later that season, but the ripple effect was everywhere apparent. We went from an organization on the rise, with a talented core of young players, to a winning organization. That was Keith's mentality, rubbing off on the rest of us.

He walked the walk—better, he *strode*—and we could only fall in behind.

Now, the inverse of this first cardinal rule telling our pitcher to keep the Red Sox off the board was the one telling our hitters to keep the pressure on, to keep piling on those runs at every chance, and as soon as Roger dispatched those three Red Sox hitters on just seven pitches our focus turned back to the choke hold we'd started to put on this game in our last turn at bat. We were helped along in this by the appearance of Calvin Schiraldi, back on the mound after his wobbly performance in Game 6, and here again I have to question John McNamara's thinking. I mean, Schiraldi had already shown his current and former teammates that he was a little overmatched by these big moments—something I could now relate to from my seat at the end of the bench. But let's be clear, a 3–3 tie, bottom of the seventh, Game 7 of the World Series was a big moment. I have to think, looking back, that the moment Schiraldi's name was announced the confidence level in our dugout went through the roof, while the confidence level across the diamond in the Boston dugout probably went through the floor—another zero-sum equation that would have left us in the plus column. In baseball, as in life, there's only so much of this confidence stuff to go around. Whatever confidence we were able to draw from this matchup had to come from somewhere, so we siphoned off what we could from our

Red Sox counterparts and counted this a good and welcome exchange.

The thing about Schiraldi was that we had a history with him, reaching back before we got to him in Game 6. Recall, he'd been a first-round draft pick for the Mets in 1983, and part of our talented core of young pitchers until he was traded to the Red Sox in the deal that brought Bobby Ojeda to Shea ahead of the 1986 season. But while Schiraldi was in the fold he rubbed a lot of guys the wrong way. One of the things we noticed was how he tried to muscle his way in to the clubhouse card games with some of the veteran players. When you were a rookie, or a second-year player, that kind of thing just wasn't done—you were meant to know your place, but Schiraldi didn't appear to think along these lines, and I believe it cost him. In subtle ways, off the field, it cost him. Guys didn't really acknowledge him in the clubhouse pecking order, the same way they did the other young pitchers on the team—Doc, Sid, Aguilera, me. Schiraldi didn't form a lot of close friendships, or fall in with any one group. He was more of a lone wolf, which is not the best way to start your major league career. Perhaps as a result, he got a reputation in our clubhouse as a second-rate member of our pitching staff. I'm not suggesting that the reputation was justified, but there it was—and it could have been completely unfair, but it seemed to stick. It got to where, as a team, we didn't trust him with the ball. It got to where, as a team, we all thought he was shaky, soft, unreliable. It was in our body language and, soon enough, it was in his.

The trade to the Red Sox was a good thing for Schiraldi— he'd become a kind of pariah in our clubhouse. It wasn't *just* about the card-playing, of course, but it was clear to everyone in and around the team that he had a lot of trouble fitting himself in, so it was felt that the change of scenery would do him good. And it did . . . for a while, until he ran into his old teammates and we started to use these first impressions against him. Invariably, it became a kind of self-fulfilling prophecy. We'd kicked Schiraldi's ass in Game 6, so naturally we all believed we would continue to kick his ass here in Game 7—that's just how ballplayers think. You learn to *smell* weakness. You look for it, feast on it. It was no longer about that softness or shakiness we'd all ascribed to Schiraldi when he pitched for the Mets. That might have been a part of it, going in to this series, but now our conviction had more to do with the fact that we'd owned him just two nights before.

We went to work on Schiraldi right away, before he had a chance to get comfortable.

Ray Knight drove a 2-1 pitch to deep left-center field for a home run to start the inning, and the place went nuts. Oh, my . . . it was like a wall of noise went up all across the city. There were reports of people honking their car horns on the Grand Central Parkway, signaling their excitement to fellow travelers as they drove past Shea. There were cabdrivers snarled in midtown traffic who leaned out their windows listening to the game. Phil Simms, the New York Giants quarterback who happened to be playing that night in the Meadowlands, told me years later how Giants fans went completely crazy as news of this Ray Knight home run began to snake its way through the stadium. People were listening to the World Series on their transistor radios, and the scoreboard operators would flash occasional updates, but here they had to stop the football game and reset the clock, there was so much noise and commotion.

Phil told me he'd never heard the place so loud—he couldn't even call a play in the huddle.

And here at Shea? Well, you could just forget about hearing yourself think. Poor Calvin Schiraldi couldn't find the plate after that Knight home run. Lenny Dykstra, pinch-hitting for Kevin Mitchell in the seventh spot in the order, was crouched so low it was as if the strike zone had all but disappeared, and Schiraldi couldn't find it for trying. All season long, Dykstra had given National League pitchers fits, the way he'd shrink the strike zone and make himself so small at the plate, and here he made himself smaller still. At 3-0, he took a called strike, but then he came back and smoked a line drive into right field for a single.

The Dykstra at bat was the perfect distillation of Lenny's peculiar blend of personality and perseverance. Lenny was the strangest, most interesting teammate I ever had. He used to give off this manic Hunter S. Thompson vibe—without the hallucinogens. You never knew *exactly* where he was coming from, and the thing of it is, Lenny himself never seemed to know *exactly* where he was coming from. He was a bundle of frenetic energy, a freak of human nature. He moved about the field, the clubhouse, the team bus like a windup toy on tilt. He was a gambler at heart, always trying to hustle up a game of cards. He'd gamble on the field, too—meaning, he'd take some huge risks, looking to make the spectacular play over the safe play. More than anyone else in our dugout, he knew that baseball was entertainment, and he played the game with this in mind. He played to win, make no mistake, but with Lenny it was all about winning with style, winning in such a way that everyone's jaw was dropped in some kind of astonishment.

Just look at this pinch-hitting appearance and break it down. Lenny had the spunk of an everyday player, so he'd been sitting on his hands during these frustrating early innings, just waiting for a chance to be let out of the gate. And here he knew his job was to get on base, rile up these Red Sox, make something happen. The way he crouched low and shrunk the strike zone when he'd worked the count to 3-0 was one of his signature moves—we used to call it his Eddie Gaedel stance, in honor of the famous little person signed by St. Louis Browns owner-showman Bill Veeck in the 1950s. (Gaedel made one plate appearance for the Browns—earning a walk on four pitches.) But Lenny didn't have the patience to wait out the walk, and when he found a pitch he liked he drove it into right field and put another dent in Schiraldi's armor.

Lenny wasn't *just* a showman, of course. Like Keith Hernandez, he was clutch to the core. Outside of Keith, he was probably one of the most clutch players I've ever seen. He had an uncanny way of getting it done—whatever *it* happened to be, whatever was called for in the moment. Realize, every player at the major league level is blessed with talent, and Lenny certainly had talent—but he *willed* himself to become a great player. That's a hard thing to do. Either you're a great player or you're not, but Lenny wouldn't accept anything short of greatness. It wasn't in his nature. He had more confidence than anyone I'd ever played with—and sometimes that confidence burst forth in unsettling ways.

Just a week earlier, in Game 3 of this series, his confidence was out in force. Remember, we'd lost the first two games at home, so we were down 2-0 and looking at two games in Fenway Park, where the Red Sox had the advantage of getting

Don Baylor into the lineup as designated hitter. But none of that mattered to Lenny, who was batting in the leadoff spot. He took up position in the on-deck circle as Oil Can Boyd completed his warm-ups, and the things Lenny was screaming toward the pitcher's mound were pretty much unprintable. He dropped every hateful, hurtful declaration he thought was suitable to the moment, along with a whole bunch of *unsuitable* comments. You have to realize, in an old ballpark like Fenway, the distance between the on-deck circle and the pitcher's mound is nothing. Lenny was practically on top of the pitcher, which made his tirade all the more remarkable. He was relentless, fearless, tasteless, running his mouth every which way. I'd never seen anything like it—really, it was remarkable. One of the themes of his venomous chatter was that this was going to be a bad, bad day for Boyd, that Lenny was going to take him deep, that we were about to put a hurt on these Red Sox like you wouldn't believe. He was taunting him mercilessly, and what was so interesting to me here was that we were up against it. We'd given away our home field advantage, down 2-0 in the series, so by rights we should have dialed down the swagger and taken more of an underdog approach, but to a man our guys would have told you it was still our series to win. Lenny was just giving voice to what we were all thinking. Loudly. Crassly. It was hubris, of the highest order. And yet it was so, so typical of Lenny, and typical of the 1986 New York Mets. Even down 2-0 in the series, we put it out there that we had the Red Sox exactly where we wanted them, that we would dictate these next games.

And do you know what? We did. Absolutely, we did, and I have to think in a lot of ways the series turned on the back of

Lenny's vitriol, before the first pitch was thrown at Fenway. It had to rattle Boyd, hearing Lenny run his mouth like that. And forget Boyd—I'm sure it pissed off the entire Red Sox bench. But Lenny did more than just talk—he also delivered. He stepped to the plate and drove a 1-1 pitch down the right-field line for a leadoff home run, so before the game was even under way, we had our edge.

That's the thing about Lenny Dykstra: he *always* delivered. Forget the troubles that would find him away from the field when his playing days were over. In his time, in his way, he was one of the most dynamic, most unique spark plugs to ever play the game, and I used to sit back and watch him and think how lucky we were to have him on our side.

If there was any doubt in that old stadium that the moment hadn't gotten to Schiraldi, it was erased with the next batter—the hardly hitting Raffy Santana. Already, Schiraldi had been paying a little too much attention to Dykstra dancing off first base—he'd thrown over a couple of times, but Lenny was really taunting him, stretching his lead, begging for a throw. Like all our teammates looking *hitterish* with their first-pitch swinging, Lenny was looking *runnerish,* like he was itching to go. That's a phrase we used to use as pitchers, and with Lenny it almost always applied. He'd stolen thirty bases on the season, so he was a constant threat to go, and here he was reminding Schiraldi of that threat as he stretched his lead and danced off the bag. To this day, I've got no idea if Lenny had the green light from Davey on this, but he was doing everything he could to make Schiraldi *think* he was going. Finally, on a 1-0 count, Rich Gedman called for a pitchout, but Schiraldi threw it so wide it went past the catcher for a wild pitch, sending Dykstra to second, and on the very next pitch Raffy slapped the ball down the first-base line, just inside the bag, just past the backhanded reach of Buckner, sending Lenny around to score.

Oh, how I wished I could have turned my cap in on itself and joined in the rally cap silliness, in the jumping around . . . but I was still yoked to those dismal early innings and ever-mindful that it was me who'd made these late-inning runs so damn meaningful. It wouldn't do for me to be whooping it up and celebrating at these twists and turns—even though, in my head, I was doing cartwheels. Even though, for the first time since I'd thrown that first pitch in the first inning, I was able to breathe.

We weren't done with Schiraldi just yet. Roger McDowell still had some work to do, and he hit for himself in what was clearly a sacrifice situation. Roger was one of the better hitters on our pitching staff, and he managed to push a near-perfect bunt to the first-base side—with two strikes!—moving Santana to second and putting Schiraldi out of his misery.

Joe Sambito came on to replace him—another former teammate, he'd appeared in eight games for the Mets the year before—and he promptly filled that open base at first with an intentional walk to Mookie. Then he moved the runners along and filled the bases with an unintentional walk to Wally Back-man, which brought Keith Hernandez back to the plate on the cusp end of one of those big moments that could bust the game wide open.

Here Keith could only drive the ball to deep center field, deep enough to score Raffy from third, but not quite the back-breaking, bases-clearing result we'd all come to expect from Keith—the result Keith had come to expect from himself.

After that, Kid had a chance to keep the inning going, but McNamara brought on Bob Stanley to face him and Gary chopped the ball to short for the last out of the inning.

Whatever had happened in those early innings, however poorly I'd pitched, we'd fought our way past it. Now it fell to Roger McDowell and the rest of our bullpen to hold on to our brand-new three-run lead.

10

REDEMPTION, OF A KIND

So here is where it would be nice to write that we shut the Red Sox down over these final innings and won the game going away. But it's never that easy, right?

Roger McDowell struggled in the top of the eighth—or maybe it just worked out that the Boston hitters had a little more fight in them and would have found a way get to *any* pitcher we sent to the mound. To Roger's great credit, he had pitched five no-hit innings in that extra-inning marathon against Houston in the playoffs just the week before—the man was gassed, and by this point Davey Johnson had ridden him just about as hard as he could.

Bill Buckner led off the inning with a slicing line drive single to short left, on a pretty inside-out swing that reminded all of us why he was such a respected hitter.

Next, Jim Rice slapped a hard single up the middle, so now there were runners on first and second, and what was interesting here was the way the crowd seemed to take it down a notch with each hit. It's like there was a volume button, and the Red Sox batters were looking to set the thing on *mute*. All that clapping and foot-stomping and cheering our lungs out . . . it had to be distracting, right? Let me tell you, Shea Stadium was rocking at the start of the inning. The fans were on their feet, but then that first hit from Buckner put a bit of a lid on the celebration—the single from Rice even moreso. And now as Dwight Evans came to bat I half expected the organist to chime in with the opening notes of Beethoven's Fifth Symphony—*dit-dit-dit-dah*—to signal the gloom-and-doom that suddenly gripped the crowd.

In the middle of all the nail-biting and tugging out of hair, I found the time to wonder why John McNamara wasn't pinch-running for Buckner at second. To be fair, to be sure, some of this second-guessing I'm offering in these pages has more than a little to do with perspective, with my long-running gig as a baseball analyst and commentator that now rivals my career as a big-league ballplayer in duration, with the ways the game has changed over the past thirty years. Still, then as now, a lot of managers would have made that switch. Yes, the Red Sox were down three runs, so that lead run didn't matter nearly as much as the tying run at the plate, but the last thing Boston wanted was to see that lead runner cut down at home, trying to score on a single. Of all the ways there are to kill a rally or a momentum run, there are few that are more spirit-crushing. Over at first base, Jim Rice wasn't much faster, so the Red Sox could have used a swifter set of wheels there, too, but Evans made the question moot when he drove a bases-clearing double to deep right field. The ball was hit deep enough that Buckner and Rice scored easily—with Rice pretty much nipping at Buckner's heels the whole way home.

Now a stunned silence seemed to blanket the stadium. We'd been dialed down to *mute*, after all. And in our dugout, where we had moments earlier been loose and merry, we were now tense and not-so-merry. I was huddled in the back corner, about as far removed from the action on the field as this sliver of New York real estate allowed, my arm draped around Sid Fernandez, my Hawaiian savior, and we went from laughing and celebrating to stewing and lamenting in the time it took Buckner and Rice to run the bases.

The mood of our concrete rectangular room was *not good*. We were caught somewhere between expecting the best and bracing for the worst.

This time of year, this big a spot, Davey Johnson wasn't about to give Roger McDowell the rope he'd need to pull himself up and out of this mess, so he brought in Jesse Orosco to face Rich Gedman. It helped that it set up a lefty-lefty matchup—Davey lived and died by the platoon, on both sides of the ball, but I have to think he would have made the move either way. We'd had this kind of dual-closer set up all season long—Roger and Jesse each had twenty-plus saves for us during the regular season—and we were able to attack these trouble spots in opposing lineups from the left side or the right.

(By the way, much would be made these days about Davey Johnson calling on Jesse Orosco to record a six-out save in this spot, but in 1986 it was just known as a save—oh, how the game has changed.)

Personally, I was always happy to see Jesse Orosco enter a

game for us—that is, I was happy when the game was under control and he was merely tasked with protecting a lead. When he had to put out a fire like the one that was threatening to ignite here, then *happy* wasn't my front-and-center emotion. *Relieved*, was more like it. *Assured* . . . that works, too. Jesse was an exceptional athlete—probably the best all-around athlete on our team. (Certainly, he was the best ballplayer I'd ever seen on a golf course—a distinction that meant a lot among the golfers on the '86 team.) He had unbelievable spin on his breaking ball—when he was on, he was impossible to read. And get this: when you'd play catch with Jesse on the field, warming up before the game, his ball would sing as it sailed past. You could hear it making a *ssss*-ing sound.

Jesse ended up pitching in the major leagues for twenty-four years, appearing in more than 1,200 games—a record. But none of us who played with him when he came up with the Mets were surprised by his longevity. He wasn't one of those guys you'd see working out all the time, but he was a natural. He could fall out of bed and pitch. And pitch. And pitch. And here we were all *relieved* to see him take the hill and start staring down Geddie at the plate. It's not that we didn't have the confidence in Roger McDowell to do the same, but it was time to stop fucking around and put this Red Sox rally on pause, and we all believed Jesse was the guy to do it.

"Job One" for Geddie in this spot was to advance the runner—that's all. McNamara wasn't about to ask him to bunt, but it was on Richie to pull the ball and give Evans a chance to cross over to third with the tying run.

"Job One" for Jesse was to keep that from happening, and he went to work on it right away. He started out with a big, sweeping curveball that dropped in on the outside corner for a called strike. Then he followed that up with another hook, almost the exact same pitch, to the exact same spot. This time, Gedman swung and missed.

Finally, on an 0-2 count, Jesse got him to float a soft liner to Wally Backman at second. It was an easy grab for Wally, and he almost doubled Evans off the bag at second, and just like that the complexion of the inning was completely changed.

Now it was Dave Henderson's job to advance the runner—only here, he had to think about advancing him all the way around. Just moving Evans to third wouldn't really improve Boston's outlook all that much if it cost the team another out, so Henderson was looking to drive the ball. It was Henderson who'd hit that tie-wounding home run off Rick Aguilera to lead off the tenth inning in Game 6, so he was a dangerous hitter in this spot—a guy who could turn this game around with a single swing of the bat. And he knew it. He was first-pitch swinging—chopped the first pitch foul. He was second-pitch swinging, too—missed, for strike two.

At 0-2, Orosco tried to get Henderson to chase a ball in the dirt, and it nearly skipped past Kid for a wild pitch, but Gary did a tremendous job keeping the ball in front of him. A play like that, it doesn't show up in the box score, it might not even get talked about in the postgame analysis. But it was big upon big upon big. And what you didn't even think about, watching Gary field his position, was what a large guy he was. He stood 6'2", weighed 210 pounds, but he was so nimble behind the plate, and here he saved us a mess of worry. If Evans crossed to third with less than two outs, all Henderson had to do was lift a ball to the outfield to tie the game—and then where would we be? As it happened, Henderson could only wave at Orosco's next pitch for strike three, and at this point the crowd was once again on its feet. We were once again cheering our collective lungs out. Whatever hesitation or nervousness we'd all been feeling was now dissipated, the momentum swung back our way.

Trouble was, Don Baylor was looming in the on-deck circle, and he came on to pinch-hit for Spike Owen. Baylor was probably the most feared designated hitter in the American League—he'd hit thirty-one home runs that year—but he hadn't really been a factor in these home games against us. Nevertheless, he was an imposing presence. Jesse started him out with a looping curve that dropped in for a called strike. Baylor was looking for a fastball, I'm sure. He was up there to hit, not to tease out a walk, so he jumped on Jesse's next pitch and grounded out to Rafael Santana at short.

Bullet dodged, but not without a couple of flesh wounds. Those two runs had been our cushion, and we'd given them away just as swiftly as we'd collected them, so now it was back on us to find a way to reclaim them.

Ah, Darryl Strawberry.

Remember when Reggie Jackson famously boasted to *Sport* magazine that he was the straw that stirred the Yankees' drink? It was back in 1977, the year he joined the Yankees, and it pissed off his new teammates, especially Thurman Munson, who'd been one of the leaders of that team. What Reggie said was this: "It all flows from me. I'm the straw that stirs the drink. Munson thinks he can be the straw that stirs the drink, but he can only stir it bad."

One of the things that made Reggie Jackson such a force and a presence was the bluster beneath that line. He had his chest out, always. No matter how big the moment, he had it in his head that he was up to it—that he was *bigger* than the moment, even. And he usually was.

The 1986 New York Mets had our own Straw, but Darryl never really stirred the drink in such a big-time way, at least not on any kind of consistent basis. In fact, I can probably count the times he rose to the occasion in a Mets uniform and lived up to the great expectations everybody seemed to have for him when he was selected with the first overall draft pick in 1980, and this right here was one of those times, leading off the bottom of the eighth.

Darryl drove an 0-2 pitch high and deep over the right-field fence with one of his beautiful, arcing swings, off of Al Nipper who had come on in relief. It was a monster shot, and it took Darryl about a month to round the bases. (Okay, so maybe I exaggerate here, but it had to have been at least a week.) It's like he was trying to savor this moment—along with the rest of us—and at the same time to rub it in to Nipper and the Red Sox, who for the second game in a row had let their World Series rings fall from their fingers.

Al Nipper didn't appreciate the super-slow home run trot. The next time he faced Darryl, in spring training the following year, he plunked him good and hard. But we appreciated it up and down our bench, because as Darryl took his sweet time touching the bases we eased our minds into the sweet reality we'd nearly let slip away in the top of the eighth: this game was ours. The heavy lifting was done. We were only three outs away.

Now, I don't mean to jump on Darryl or to blow up his spot in this account, because there's no denying that this was a big-time moment. It wasn't exactly a *game-changing* moment, but it was certainly a *game-cementing* one and, just then, this was just as big. And, just then, it wasn't *just* the home run that put a flourish on this game, it was the boastfulness underneath it. It was in Darryl's arrogant home run trot—it put it out there that we would not be denied, the professional equivalent of taking our dog-chewed ball from the sandlot and heading home.

That said, I believe it's important to place this big moment in context, alongside the other big moments that never really found Darryl in a Mets uniform—again, not in any kind of consistent way. Straw, at his best, was one of the most feared hitters in the game. He could run, throw, hit, and cover all kinds of ground in the outfield. By every measure, he should have had a gargantuan career; instead, he had a really solid career. A lot of times, he was painted with the same brush as Dwight Gooden—the media liked to throw them together, but the reality was they didn't hang out all that much. I don't think they liked each other, really. Dwight was a sweet, good-natured kid. *Sweet* wouldn't have been one of the top-ten words you'd use to describe Darryl's makeup. He was more hard than sweet.

The two of them made their own separate troubles, and it wouldn't be fair for me to dwell on those troubles here. To their great credit, they've each copped to their drug abuse and reckless behavior since leaving the game, and they've gotten their shit together. That's fantastic, I'm happy for them, pulling for them, but the reason I'm taking this mini-swipe at

Darryl here is for what his career could have been. No question, the guy was an exceptionally gifted athlete, but he didn't work very hard at his game. Because of this, he wasn't the easiest guy to have around as your teammate. You'd be busting your ass, doing everything you could to get and keep in shape, to get and keep a step ahead of your opponent, and there was Darryl, coasting, phoning it in, and still managing to hit 335 home runs in his career, with an even 1,000 RBI.

At the end of the day, at the ends of their careers, Gooden and Strawberry should have put up numbers to rival Clemens and Bonds. Doc should have had 300 wins. Darryl should have hit 700 home runs. But they didn't even come close, and the further away I am from my playing days, the more I resent how they squandered their gifts—but hey, they were *their* gifts to squander, not mine; *their* choices to make, not mine. At the time, I suppose I resented it a little more in Darryl, because Doc had that sweetness about him. Doc was like a lost kid. Darryl, at times, didn't seem to give a shit.

And I resented it, too, because we were all pulling on the same chain. We were supposed to be a team, right? When one guy didn't pull his weight, it made it that much tougher on the rest of us, so it was hard to root for Darryl. He came through for us here—really, it's like he drove a stake through the heart of that Red Sox team with his magnificent home run, with his arrogant home run trot—but in memory the moment loses some of its shine because of the career that came with it.

There were just a couple of obstacles left in our path.

First, there was the messy business of celebration for the grounds crew to get past. For some reason, Mets fans that year were fond of hurling toilet paper rolls from the upper deck. It was good, harmless fun, and I've got to admit those toilet paper streamers looked way cool as the rolls unfurled as they fell to the field, but it was a huge pain in the ass. Here, it held things up for a few long moments as the paper was cleared from the field, and in that time we whipped ourselves into a whole new frenzy. We'd been down, then up, then up again, then down a little ... and now here we were, all the way up.

When play resumed, Ray Knight went up the middle on an 0-2 pitch to continue the rally Straw had started.

Lenny Dykstra, who'd remained in the game in center field after pinch-hitting for Kevin Mitchell in the seventh, moving Mookie Wilson over to Mitchell's spot in left, worked his way to another 3-1 count before grounding out to Ed Romero, who'd come in on a double-switch after Don Baylor pinch-hit for Spike Owen.

Ray Knight advanced to second on the play, so we had another runner in scoring position, with one out.

Next, McNamara had Nipper walk Santana intentionally, probably trying to force Davey Johnson's hand, since Jesse Orosco was due to follow in the pitcher's spot in the order.

But Davey wasn't about to lift Jesse for a pinch hitter. For one thing, it was a clear sacrifice situation, and Jesse could handle the bat well. As a reliever, he didn't get to bat all that often, but he'd collected his share of hits. We still had Kevin Elster, Howard Johnson, and Danny Heep on the bench, but it was clear to everyone in the dugout that Davey wanted to go into battle in the ninth with his go-to closer, especially since he'd already *gone to* his other closer, and since Wade Boggs was due to bat second in the inning and Davey liked that lefty-lefty matchup.

Jesse squared to bunt and laid off on the first pitch from Nipper, which sailed high. By laying off like that, we had a chance to see the Boston infield on the move—Boggs and Buckner pinching in and charging on the corners, Romero and Barrett rotating toward third and first to cover the bags. Second pitch, same thing, only here Nipper got the ball over the plate.

At 1-1, the Red Sox were expecting Jesse to square around to bunt yet again—and, frankly, most everyone in the Mets dugout was expecting the same—but as Boggs and Buckner inched toward home, as Romero and Barrett rolled to the corners, Jesse pulled the bat back and swung away, chopping the ball up the middle where the shortstop was meant to be.

Knight came around to score, restoring our cushion to the three-run lead we enjoyed going into the eighth, and whipping the crowd into a whole new frenzy.

That was all for Al Nipper, who gave way to Steve Crawford, who'd gotten spanked in Game 4—he gave up a two-run homer to Lenny Dykstra, and another dinger to Gary Carter, among other missteps.

It looked like Crawford was still feeling those postseason jitters, because he drilled Mookie Wilson in the foot to load the bases. Mookie jumped to get out of the way of the pitch, but the ball caught him in such a way that it seemed to trip him up, and he spun to the ground like a seven-pin clipped by Earl Anthony to make the spare. (Historians take note: Mookie's acrobatics would *not* have served us just two nights before, because if he'd gotten clipped by a similar pitch that got away from Bob Stanley in Game 6, his at bat would have ended before Mookie had a chance to send that historic dribbler down the first-base line.)

With the infield in, Wally Backman hit a broken bat tapper to Marty Barrett, who was playing in on the grass at second, and Marty made a strong throw to Gedman to force Santana.

That brought Keith Hernandez to the plate, hitting with the bases loaded for the third straight time. Here again, the crowd went wild, or wilder still. You could see Mex licking his chops at the thought of piling on. Really, he was like the wolf in those old Looney Tunes cartoons, salivating, savoring the moment. He was seeing the ball well that night, had hit the ball hard each time up, but here he hit a sinking line drive to Barrett, who short-hopped the ball and made the throw to first for the third out of the inning.

Keith was pissed, but only a little. He was a gamer, but he was also a professional, and here he could see that it didn't much matter. A three-run lead was more than enough to see us through. The Boston Red Sox were defeated, deflated . . . *done*.

Some loose thoughts from the ninth inning and beyond . . .

I remained huddled with Sid Fernandez in the back corner of the dugout, at the far end of the bench, our own little island state. That's where we'd been since Sid left the game and we began our comeback, and we weren't moving anytime soon. Even as the dugout began to fill with police officers and stadium security, with New York City Mayor Ed Koch and other dignitaries, with reporters, we stuck to our spot.

There was good karma there, especially beneath the clamor

of a couple hundred fans in the front rows just above, banging on the dugout roof like it was a great big drum, rattling those old Shea bones.

Someone asked for a book on Ed Romero, who was due to lead off, and then another someone said there was no need for a book on Ed Romero. Really, there wasn't. Nothing against Ed Romero, but he was a light-hitting shortstop—that's all Jesse Orosco needed to know, and he went after him like Romero had no business standing in at the plate, top of the ninth inning, Game 7 of the World Series. Romero was overmatched, I think. He popped up in foul territory on the first-base side, and Sid and I watched as Jesse, Keith, and Kid circled underneath. It was Keith's play to make, and he did, but the ball was tailing away from him and he had to lunge for it at the last moment.

One down.

Wade Boggs was next—the lefty-lefty matchup Davey wanted, and here it felt to me like Jesse could do no wrong out there on that hill. It's like the moment was built for him, like he was built for the moment, and even the leading hitter in the American League could not get in the way of that moment. Boggs grounded out to Wally Backman at second on a 1-2 pitch.

Two down.

Next thing I noticed, someone had tossed a smoke bomb from the stands. I didn't see it land, but a giant plume of deep red smoke suddenly mushroomed out in left field. It's a wonder Mookie Wilson wasn't hit, wasn't hurt. Time was called. There wasn't a whole lot of wind, so the red smoke seemed to hang in the still night air for the longest time, and in the waiting the boisterous crowd went crazier still. The fans stepped up their toilet paper tossing, and I looked out at the scene, thick smoke hanging low above the outfield grass, toilet paper streamers sailing every which way, dozens of New York City police officers on horseback lining up in the bullpens, and thought we were in the middle of a strange battlefield.

The game was delayed for about five minutes—a long time to have to wait to throw up your arms in inevitable celebration. And it *did* seem inevitable just then. Even in the Boston dugout, from where Sid and I sat, I could see looks of resignation.

Finally, after just shy of forever, the smoke dissipated and play resumed with Marty Barrett at the plate—Boston's last hope, the Red Sox's best hitter for these series games. But Marty was no match for the "Let's Go Mets!" energy in that stadium. He was no match for the long slog of a season we'd just endured.

At 2-2, Sid and I left our seats and moved once again to the top step of the dugout, this time to watch Jesse punch Barrett out with a fastball upstairs.

I don't remember too much after that.

I do remember running onto the field and dive-bombing into the scrum of players that formed around the mound.

I do remember exchanging hugs and high-fives and *can-you-fuckin'-believe-its!* with my Mets teammates, coaches, trainers.

I do remember watching those mounted policemen line up along the perimeter of the field and taking the time to wonder who was the low man on the grounds crew totem pole, because he'd be the one cleaning up all that horseshit. (And now, all these years later, I catch myself wondering at the symmetry of this moment—the horseshit being left on the field by these *actual* horses standing in for the horseshit I'd left on this same field just a couple of hours earlier.)

I do remember spilling into the clubhouse and thinking for a moment that the stadium was about to collapse on us. You could feel the place rocking and rumbling and cracking at the seams.

I do remember the sweet sting of champagne when it got into my eyes, and how cold it felt dripping down my back.

I do remember having the presence of mind to alert our clubhouse manager Charlie Samuels that he should probably move the piles of provocative mail that came in for us from "Baseball Annie" types who'd send in their bras and panties, their suggestive photos, their lurid proposals. A lot of the wives and families were coming into the clubhouse to join in our celebration, and I remember thinking there was no reason for them to have to walk past piles of all that interesting stuff.

I do remember how Rich Gedman had the class and character to come looking for me after the game to offer his congratulations—Rich Gedman, who grew up the same way I did, in the same time, in the same place, rooting for the same Red Sox, with the same hopes and blue-collar dreams. It had to be tough for him, to be so close to a championship and to see it run away from him—tougher, still, to suck it up and seek me out to shake my hand and wish me well. And to this day I remember how I looked right past him—in my lame-ass defense, because I didn't really recognize him out of uniform, our battle armor stripped away, but also because I wasn't really focused on what this moment might have meant for him. Oh, I shook his hand (at least, I *think* I shook his hand. . . . I *hope*

I shook his hand), but I didn't take the time to acknowledge our special connection, to give him the respect he deserved.

I remember heading back out to the field, to the mound, and sitting with a bunch of my teammates—Rick Aguilera, Howard Johnson, Wally Backman—and swilling champagne. Toasting the crowd. Drinking in the moment. Roughhousing, same way I used to do with my brothers, imagining ourselves into our own championship celebrations. Wanting this night to never, ever end. Wishing like crazy I could forget how it started.

11

THE MORNING AFTER

It took awhile getting out of Shea, but there was a party to be made, and we made it at a celebrity joint called Columbus on the Upper West Side. I went with my parents, with my wife, Toni, with Keith Hernandez and his girlfriend and, strangely, with Robert De Niro and his son Raphael, and a young Mike Tyson, just a month or so before his first title fight. It was a great night, in the company of this wonderfully odd collection of variously interconnected people. That's how it goes in a city like New York, when you're at the center of the swirl, all eyes on you and yours. At some point, Bobby Ojeda joined our traveling party, and some of my brothers flitted in and out, and I remember being struck by the absurd mix at our table. I wasn't so fully in the moment that the moment didn't register.

Just to put it in context, let's remember that De Niro was already a two-time Academy Award winner and New York City icon, and that in a short time Iron Mike would become the most famous heavyweight boxer of his generation. There was a lot of "juice" at our table, but the unsettling truth was that most of it was coming from me and Keith.

There was a real pecking order at Columbus, which was one of our regular hangouts during the season. Typically, there were A-list tables, and B-list tables, and C-list tables, and on most nights the Manhattan-based Mets took a seat on some middle ground. At the start of the season, my teammates and I were sometimes afterthoughts among the Columbus crowd, depending on what else was going on. On this night, though, we were the headliners, and the Columbus faithful seemed to want to lean into our group and join in our celebration. For the first time, I understood what it meant to be the toast of the town because, let's face it, for this one night at least, we were A-Number-One, head of the list, cream of the crop, top of the heap.

Throughout the night, in the corner of my eye, I could see my mother gabbing happily with Mike Tyson, and I caught myself wondering what the hell they were talking about, laughing about, but there they were talking, laughing. Like this sort of thing happened all the time, instead of hardly ever—my mother, yukking it up with a street-tough Brooklyn boxer. And all the while, folks were sending over drinks, lifting their glasses, doing what they could to lubricate our little celebration.

Let me tell you, it was a good and wonderful thing, to be on the receiving end of such genuine good cheer, and from the way the party was gathering steam, it didn't look like we'd run out of that good cheer anytime soon.

I wouldn't say it was a *wild* night in the bacchanalian sense because, after all, *my parents were there*. Because, after all, it's tough to cut loose when there are so many sets of eyes on you. But it was wild in that hard-to-fathom way—meaning, it was a difficult picture to get my head around. Me, hobnobbing with these beautiful people. Me, at the center of all this attention. Me, able to forget for these few wee-hour moments the disappointment I'd felt when I'd been knocked from that pitching mound by those Red Sox hitters. To be completely honest, my miserable performance weighed on me long after we'd popped our last bottle of champagne. It gnawed at me that I had somehow stepped into this rare sliver of spotlight and failed to deliver under the weight of what were admittedly great expectations. Yes, my teammates had bailed me out. Yes, the destiny we'd all felt had been somehow attached to our group all season long had somehow wiped the slate clean and made us all champions. But it almost felt to me like I didn't belong in the middle of all these back-slaps and huzzahs. I hadn't *earned* these congratulations, after all.

This disconnect dogged me all the way back to my apartment, and kept me tossing and turning most of the night. I didn't sleep much, although I suppose this had to do with a whole mess of emotions and the adrenaline high that I'm sure found each of us on that team, in our own way. It wasn't necessarily that I'd let my teammates down, that I'd let Mets fans down, that I'd let *myself* down, but there was just so much *stuff* bouncing around in my head, I had some trouble keeping it all straight. I was fidgety, restless. And it didn't help that my parents were early risers—early, as in *crack of dawn*. For as long as I could remember, my father was headed out to work by 4:30 in the morning, and I guess his body clock had him up with the sun. It didn't help that my parents were deathly afraid of New York—really, they absolutely hated the city—so I'm sure my father had been sleeping with one eye open, and as soon as the sounds of early morning street life began to awaken the neighborhood, he was up and at it.

By the way, my parents were sleeping on a futon I'd had delivered just a few days prior to the start of the World Series, once I knew they'd be coming to town for these games, and I found out some years later that it had been delivered by the actor and comedian Ray Romano, back before his stand-up career had taken off. Ray was a lifelong Mets fan—remember, he named his brother's bulldog Shamsky on *Everybody Loves Raymond,* after my good friend and 1969 World Champion Met Art Shamsky—so I guess it made an impression when he saw my name on the delivery ticket, and even more of an impression when I tipped him $20. He said once in an interview that it was the best tip he ever got delivering futons, so I guess it really was a championship season, all around.

After a while, with my parents clambering about the small apartment, I gave up on the pretense of sleep, so we all sat around waiting for the time we had to leave for the ticker-tape parade downtown. The plan was for us to take the subway, which didn't sit all that well with my parents, who half believed the bowels of the city were rife with criminals and monsters, but it was tough to keep track of the road closings or to anticipate the traffic, so we didn't have a whole lot of options. Trouble was, everyone in the city seemed to have been heading downtown on their own version of the same idea. The first downtown train that pulled into the Thirty-fourth Street station near my apartment was packed tight. Although when the doors opened, some of the sardines inside recognized me and invited me to wedge myself in alongside, but there wasn't room enough for our entire group so we let the train pass. The second train . . . same story. Finally, after the third overcrowded train arrived, we decided to head back upstairs and try our luck on the street but, of course, there were no cabs. That's the way it was in New York City, in the days before Uber. Whenever it rained, you couldn't find a cab for trying and, apparently, whenever you needed to get to City Hall to attend a ticker tape parade in your honor, the same rule applied.

Eventually, an "off duty" cabbie took pity on us, or maybe he recognized me and picked us up for the story. Anyway, he managed to ferry us as far as he could before the police barricades blocked our path, and by "ferry" I mean to suggest that we were headed for the Staten Island Ferry terminal at the tip of Manhattan, where the parade was meant to start. We got as far south as Houston Street, I believe, before we spilled out of the cab and started the rest of the way on foot—a half mile or so, but a real crawl on this day of days. The sidewalks were choked with pedestrians, so we made our progress in the middle of the street. (Newspaper accounts would later estimate that there were more than three million people lining the parade route, so even though there were no cars it was slow going.) Despite our early start, we were now running late, so by the time we reached the terminal there was some preliminary parade activity heading *up* Broadway, which put us in the strange position of walking *against* the flow.

The upshot was that I had two parades, really—one headed downtown, on foot, just me and my family, and another one headed uptown, soon enough, in an open car, with the rest of the team. Here again, I was charmed by the warm response from the crowd. With each step, with each new segment of *throng,* I was met anew by a rush of warmth and good feeling, as if these die-hard fans had *felt* my pain the night before and were determined to help me rise above it. Really, the way I'd left the game with my head hung low, the way I'd dug a hole for us, I half expected to be met by jeers and raspberries, but Mets fans are a forgiving bunch, then as now. They seemed to suffer *with* me when I got the hook, not *against* me, and what mattered to them was that we'd come out on top. What mattered was that I'd made my meaningful contributions throughout the season, and earlier in this postseason. And so the cheers that found me as I walked against the parade traffic were for my body of work and not for this one lousy outing, and they lifted me along this canyon of heroes, headed in the wrong direction, of course.

I should mention here that I wasn't the only one running late. One of our marquee players didn't make it to the parade at all, it turned out. Doc Gooden, we all learned later, was famously holed up in his drug dealer's apartment, too wired and paranoid to join his teammates and face the crush of Mets fans lining the streets of downtown Manhattan. He wrote about his absence in his book, so I'm not pulling back the curtain on a scene Doc hasn't already revealed, but at the time we didn't need a public confession to tell us what we already knew. This was just Doc at the front end of his spiral—flashing an unpredictable streak that would come to characterize his time in our shared spotlight in predictable ways.

In fact, before the curtain went up on our season as reigning champions, Doc would be arrested for fighting with police in Tampa, and later test positive for cocaine during spring training. To avoid suspension, he entered a rehabilitation clinic, but did not rejoin the team until early June. As it turned out, it was the first of many derailments to ransack our pitching staff as we tried to defend our title in that doomed 1987 season—injuries, mostly. Sid Fernandez went down with a knee injury. Roger McDowell hurt his knee, too. Rick Aguilera had elbow problems that cost him a couple of months. Bobby Ojeda chopped off the tip of his finger while trimming the hedges at his Port Washington home. David Cone, who'd joined us in the off-season in a trade for Ed Hearn and Rick Anderson, suffered a broken thumb. And, on September 11, 1987, in the fat middle of a pennant race that still had us vying for the top spot in the National League Eastern Division despite all these setbacks, I jammed my pitching thumb trying to field a bunt off the bat of the speedy Cardinals outfielder Vince Coleman. I'd taken a no-hitter into the sixth inning, and we were nursing a three-run lead, so even though I had no chance against the fleet-footed Coleman, I dove for the ball and tried to make a highlight-reel type play.

In the end, I managed to avoid a trip to the disabled list, but only because it was September and the rosters had been expanded. For my troubles, I had a rod put in my thumb, where it still resides today. It doesn't bother me much, but I know it's there, and on the days it bothers me even a little I'm taken back to how things were for me as I left the mound that night in October 1986—my long dreamed-about Game 7 appearance in shambles. It's like a rod had been put in my boyhood fantasies, and I could only lean on it for support. Without it, I might have crumbled beneath the size of my failure, the flag of my hopes and dreams bunched at my feet. With it, I could find a way to raise that flag and let it flap in the breeze and join my teammates as a champion.

No, it wasn't how I'd imagined it, like, a million times over. It wasn't the storybook ending I would have written for myself. But here it was . . . here it was.

Back to the parade.

I wasn't meant to be in the lead car, so it's not like I'd missed my ride. No, the lead cars were for our All-Stars, our manager, our World Series MVP. If Game 7 had gone another way—if it had gone *my* way—I would have been up front, but my pitching line left me in the middle of the procession. As we arrived late to the scene there was a New York City police officer waiting to drive us back the way we came in a sweet Mustang convertible. My parents sat in the backseat, and I sat with my brother Charlie on the shelf just behind, our legs splayed out on the seat alongside our parents, like we were just a little too cool for the room.

(And we were!)

Let me tell you, if you've never been driven through a pulsing, pressed-together crowd of screaming Mets fans lining the streets of the Manhattan like the mayor was giving something away, the air thick with ticker tape and the full-throated cries of bottled-up jubilation . . . then you haven't experienced what it means to be celebrated as a champion in a city like New York. You haven't tasted what we tasted—a bit of pandemonium, mixed with a healthy dose of chaos, and sprinkled with a whole lot of bedlam. My poor parents, already leery of the big city and its denizens, were caught somewhere between fear and disbelief at the hero's welcome we kept receiving as we snake-lined up Broadway toward City Hall. Understand, those words *we kept receiving* are carefully chosen, because with each new car length, with each new stretch of street, there was a whole new subset of screams, a new rainfall of ticker tape. It was crazy—just crazy—but it was an endless loop of craziness, because as we rolled through the streets we were being greeted each time as if for the first time. The celebration kept finding us anew—again and again, over and over, first on this corner, and then on this next corner, and on and on.

At one point, I leaned to my father and whispered in his ear. I said, "Just like that time in Little League, huh?"

What I meant was that it was *kinda, sorta* like the time our Millbury team was treated like local heroes after a tough 4–1 loss in the regional tournament to a team from Newbury-port. A win would have earned us a spot in the Little League World Series, so we were a heartbroken bunch. We'd come up against a pitcher we just couldn't hit—first time we'd ever faced a kid pitcher who could throw a legit curve ball. It was a weekend afternoon game, not too far from home, so of course all of our parents had come to see us play, together with a lot of our neighbors and grandparents and aunts and uncles and cousins, and as we drove back to Millbury, still in our uniforms, it was somehow decided that we would all meet at Windle Field in the center of town. There we were met with a grand welcome—a welcome that was really more of a consolation prize, because of course we were all so disappointed, frustrated. But all these people had turned out, together with a fleet of fire trucks all spit-shined and gleaming, the way I remember it. We climbed onto those trucks and we were driven around like conquering heroes, waving to the milling-about crowds as we crisscrossed the streets of Millbury at ten miles per hour.

The streets were lined with people—maybe not the same *crush* of people I could see on either side of Broadway, but to a little kid, licking his wounds after a decent, hopeful run in the regional tournament, the moment was just as big, just as loud, just as wonderful. It's one of the great memories of my growing up, the way those fire trucks started this impromptu parade, the way all these other cars fell in behind us, the way a band turned out to play for us, the way people were honking their horns, cheering. In my head, I've always imagined that if you took an aerial shot of the scene it would have looked like that grace-note moment at the end of *Field of Dreams,* where the camera pulls back and reveals this miles-long line of cars, descending on that beautiful diamond cut into the Iowa corn-field, but, of course, it was only a little bit like that, and only in my little-kid head.

I was eleven years old, still had another year to go in my Little League career, so it was a big deal for me to be playing shortstop on this team of mostly twelve-year-olds. I naively assumed I would be back in this same spot the following year, with another chance at Williamsport, but that's not always how it goes, right? As hard as you might work, as much as you might be deserving, you never know when the stars will align and light your way to a championship, and now here I was, fifteen years later, riding in just the second parade of my baseball career, connecting the dots from how things were back then to how they were just now, and the picture that came back to me was a sweet, sure line that carried the same lies I'd told myself at eleven years old:

Take it in, Ronnie. Cherish this moment. But if you miss something, don't sweat it, because you'll be back here before too long.

Yeah, right . . .

My father must have been thinking of those fire trucks, too, because his face was suddenly lit with this microburst of dad pride and wistful nostalgia, and whatever apprehensions he'd been having about being in the eye of this particular storm, on these not-so-mean streets seemed to fall away. It was 1971 all over again, and we were all back in that moment in Millbury, falling in behind those fire trucks, looking out at our cheering community, our world a place where anything good could happen at any moment.

It was exponentially different, but *kinda, sorta* the same.

My father turned back toward me and said, "You remember that, R.J.?"

(In my family, in my neighborhood, I'd always been R.J.— Ronald Maurice Darling Jr., named for my father.)

I said, "Sure do." Like I could ever forget.

And then my father laughed, made a little thumbs-up gesture, and turned back to face the crowds. Either he didn't want to miss a thing, or he still didn't trust these nutjob New Yorkers, crushed so close together, determined to get close to whatever it was we'd all just accomplished. He wasn't driving, but he'd taken his eyes off the road to share this small, wistful memory, and now he needed to get back to it.

Somehow, our little snake line reached to City Hall, where the crowd was even bigger, even louder. There was just a great teeming mass of people shoehorned onto the street, on the plaza, leaning from the open windows of these great old office buildings and looking down on the scene. I was like a kid again—eleven years old, chasing my brother into City Hall and up the stairwell, trying to find one of those open windows. We must have been following someone, because I can't imagine we'd set off in this way on our own, but there we were, ducking in and out of these cavernous offices, where the work of the city government seemed to have been put on pause. No one was at their desks. Everyone was at the windows, or on the plaza below, and after ducking into a few of these offices we finally made our way to a big open window and craned our necks. From this vantage point, three or four stories above the crowd, the view was just incredible. There were people everywhere—a sea of happy, cheering people, stretching all the way downtown, uptown, across town.

I'd never seen so many people, couldn't even *conceive* of so many people. It's like a dozen sold-out Shea Stadiums had let out onto this scene, and I stuck my head out that window and started chanting "Let's go Mets!"—something I'd never done before, and something I never did again, but in this moment, leading our adoring fans in celebration felt pretty damn euphoric.

At some point, Mayor Koch stepped to the microphone they'd set up and started to do his "How'm I doin'?" schtick, and I took that as my cue to rejoin my teammates, and as I raced down those stairs it finally occurred to me that this was what it felt like to be a world champion. This was what it felt like to matter, in the end. As a professional athlete, you don't always allow yourself time to appreciate the brass ring you spend your whole life trying to reach. The beauty of the game, when you're in the moment, is in the pursuit. It's not until the moment has passed that you have a chance to reflect on whatever it is that you've accomplished, and those reflections take on a different hue over time.

Here is something: when you put together a championship season of Shakespearean proportions like we did in 1986, you exist in the minds of many as if in a freeze-frame. You play 162 games at a turbo level, well ahead of the pack, but then you stumble and nearly fall before you set things right and find a way to win, as if winning had been your due. It was fairly epic, the ups and downs and twists and turns of this postseason run. It was a season for the ages, but when a season for the ages happens, you are set in stone. You are a band of brothers, forever bound. Baseball fans, particularly those hued in the orange and blue tones of the Mets, tend to think of you at *just* that age, in *just* that moment, surrounded by *just* those people with whom you shared *just* this one piece of glory. But it's not like that, is it? As professional ballplayers, we were off on our own journeys, riding individual careers that would splinter off in a whole bunch of directions here on in.

It simply worked out that we all came together in this magical way for this one glorious summer.

It simply worked out that we put our heads and our hearts together and fought back to take these final games.

And because it worked out we are remembered *as we were*—not *as we are*. We might be joined for all eternity in the highlight reels of memory, but in reality we no longer see each other much—at least, not in any kind of organic way. It's the way of the game. Think about it: we're thrown together, we develop close friendships that seem to flourish in the bunker mentality of team sports, all of us working toward a common goal. We make our marks, in this indelible way. And then life happens . . . *baseball* happens . . . and we move off along our separate paths.

Truth be told, I only developed three close friendships from my time in a Mets uniform—and only one of those took root during this championship season. Now, part of that might be on me. I'm not a close-friendship kind of guy. I have a lot of loose relationships, a lot of pals, a lot of guys I can hang with, grab a beer with, watch a ballgame with, but not a whole lot of people who are a part of my life in a fundamental, day-to-day sort of way, outside of my family.

These days a lot of folks assume that Keith Hernandez and I are tight, and we are, but our friendship has transcended our time as teammates. As players, I looked up to Keith. I have a great deal of respect for him, I enjoy his company, and I will always appreciate the many kindnesses he showed me when I was a young ballplayer. As a savvy veteran, he took me under his wing, taught me the nuances of the game, the rhythms of the big city. Most of the guys on that team lived on Long Island, so Keith and I ended up spending a lot of time together since we both lived in Manhattan. We both enjoyed a good meal, a good glass of wine, a good book. We could talk about things other than baseball. But once we were no longer teammates, we drifted away from each other, not because we'd had a falling out so much as a falling away. Oh, we continued to seek each other out when we were in each other's swirl, when the game would take us to each other's ballpark, each other's city, but it's not like I was on Keith's speed dial. Now that we're back working together—teammates again!—we've picked up where we left off, and I think we both get a kick out of the fact that we're knitted together by the threads of this 1986 championship team. We might go out for dinner once in a while when we're on the road, and yet we mostly keep to ourselves away from the ballpark. We get along great, have a ton of shared history, but that's where it ends for us. He's family—enough said.

Those close friendships? Well, the first was with Ed Lynch, whose Mets tenure started a couple of years ahead of mine. He was my first friend on the team, and we've kept it up in all the years since. A lot of folks forget that Ed began the 1986 season on the Mets pitching staff, after a solid 1985 season as one of our starters. But he hurt his knee in his first appearance of the season, and never made his way back into the fold. The Mets ended up trading him to the Chicago Cubs, where he finished his career and went on to become the team's general manager, but even as we went our separate ways we managed to keep in constant touch.

The second, David Cone, was traded to the Mets just before the 1987 season. For whatever reason, Coney and I hit it off, and we still talk all the time, especially now that he's working across town, calling the games in the Yankee booth for the YES Network.

The third friendship was with Kevin Elster, who occupied an unusual spot on the 1986 team. He was a light-hitting defensive replacement for our light-hitting defensive shortstop, Rafael Santana. Kevin would go on to become a good big-league hitter—in 1996, he'd hit 24 homers and drive in 99 runs for the Texas Rangers!—but back in 1986 he was just twenty-two years old, right out of school. He was a September call-up for us that year, after being a heralded second-round pick in the 1984 amateur draft, but that just shows the depth and determination of this team. Kevin had a tremendous glove. He was arguably the best defensive shortstop I ever played with, probably just a notch below the Wizard, Ozzie Smith, on the other side of the ball. Kevin was one of the only "big" shortstops I'd ever seen who played "small"—by that I mean, at 6'2", close to 200 pounds, he had the size and stature of a Cal Ripken Jr., but he roamed the field like a little guy. He was supersmooth, agile, quick. Kevin had thighs like Eric Heiden, the great speed skater—that's how he was built. And yet he had the best glove in the organization, with incredibly soft hands and tremendous range, and as he blossomed as a player the guys on the staff would love to get the ball on days when Kevin was playing behind us in the field.

Raffy, too, was an exceptional glove man, but Kevin earned a spot on the postseason roster because Davey knew there'd be times he'd have to pinch-hit for Raffy in a close game, and he didn't want to give anything up defensively.

And so, out of this great, career-defining season, there emerged only three career-surviving friendships. One, with a guy who barely made it out of spring training that year before going on the disabled list and then being traded away. One, with a guy who joined our ranks *after* our storied championship run—even though he stuck around for a good long while after that and became a key teammate of most of the guys on the 1986 roster. And one, with a guy who played just nineteen games for us during the regular season. And yet, for me, these were the takeaway relationships from those great Mets teams.

Still, when those 1986 Mets get together for a special event, an anniversary celebration, a memorabilia signing, the fans are inclined to think of us as a unit. Even we players have been conditioned to think along these same lines.

When we're together, we're twenty-five, twenty-six years old.

When we're together, we're invincible.

When we're together, we're bound by these magical games, by the lift and roar of those great Shea crowds.

When we're together, we're champions.

Now, contrast these freeze-frame relationships with the somewhat more enduring friendships I was lucky enough to build later on in my career, after I was traded to the Oakland Athletics. In 1992, the A's made it to Game 6 of the American League Championship Series, before losing to the Toronto Blue Jays—a disappointing end to what should have been a championship season. We had a great team that year: Mark McGwire, Carney Lansford, Rickey Henderson, Harold Baines, Willie Wilson, Jose Canseco. On the mound we had Dave Stewart, Mike Moore, Bob Welch, and Dennis Eckersley out in the bullpen. It was an amazing bunch, with Tony La Russa at the helm, and up and down that lineup it was a closer group of guys than any team I'd ever been on. Why? Well, La Russa fostered a kind of collegial atmosphere, and it certainly helped that we all lived in and around Alameda County, about a fifteen-minute drive from the stadium. In New York, by comparison, we were spread all over the damn place—Long Island, Connecticut, New Jersey, the city—so we never got together away from the stadium. In Oakland, we got together all the time, usually as a full team, usually for barbecues at one another's houses, with our wives and kids. We'd play Wiffle ball, drink beer, eat chicken, hang. I suppose it helped that I was at a different stage of life when I played out in Oakland; I was married with children, with almost ten years of big-league experience, so I welcomed this kind of setup, this kind of camaraderie. I was more open to these types of friendships. And I loved the fact that the guys would talk baseball at these get-togethers. They cared about the history of the game, the strategy, the nuts and bolts—so I got off on that.

But baseball fans don't really think of that Oakland A's team the same way they think of the 1986 Mets. Certainly, Oakland fans don't think of their A's the same way New York fans think of their Mets. Why? Because the Oakland A's didn't win the World Series in 1992. We don't get together on round-numbered anniversaries to celebrate the accomplishments of that team, the way we do in New York, because in the end that team didn't *accomplish* anything, so even though I might feel more of a connection to Lansford and Eck and those guys, I'm more *connected* to Gary and Keith, Doc and Straw, Lenny and Mookie.

There's a legacy that grows on the back of a world championship, and out of that legacy there is history and moment and the points of connection that take us back, again and again, to a time long ago.

Now, as I write this, I've had thirty years to deal with the disappointment of my Game 7 performance. From time to time, I've caught myself wondering if, in an alternate universe, my life and career might have played out differently had this game played out in some other way. If we ended up losing that game on the back of my performance, I have to think it would have shortened my time in New York. Mets fans wouldn't remember my tenure with quite the same levels of warmth and good cheer. And then, on the flip side of that, if I'd managed to put together another dominant start and set us up to win the series going away, then maybe my career would have taken on a whole new flavor. Maybe it would have elevated me to the kind of platform Madison Bumgarner now occupies in the minds of San Francisco Giants fans, after giving up just one run in twenty-one innings against the Kansas City Royals in the 2014 World Series—a postseason performance for all time. Maybe I would have supplanted Doc Gooden as the ace of our staff, and gotten Davey Johnson to stop riding me once and for all.

And if we didn't find a way to erase that early deficit and find a way to win? Maybe I would have been run from the game and forced to take a job on Wall Street, and once in a while some diehard would approach me in a bar downtown, each of us dressed in our snappy power suits, and say, "Didn't you used to be Ron Darling?"

Maybe, maybe, maybe . . . who can say how things would have gone?

All I know is I've had thirty years to rethink my approach and kick myself in the ass. Thirty years to chase the dogged nightmare of what might have been and focus instead on the beautiful dream of what there was instead. Thirty years to turn the memory of that World Series from bittersweet to just plain sweet. And I'm still working on it.

It helps that I continue to hear from fans who share their own memories about that season, about the World Series, and it helps that those stories don't *always* make mention of how I was chased from that Game 7. In fact, most of them don't—like the guy who came up to me at a fund-raiser to thank me for helping him to buy his house.

I wasn't sure I'd heard him right. I said, "What?"

He explained to me he'd been a hard-core gambler as a younger man, and that in 1986 he'd had a good feeling about me and bet big on every one of my starts. Then he reminded me that I'd made thirty-eight starts that year—thirty-four in the regular season and four in the postseason—and that the Mets had won twenty-nine of them.

He said, "You were *the man* that year, Ronnie!"

And so he bought his house—the house that Darling built!—and quit gambling, and found a way to tell me what that season meant to him, what it meant to him *still*.

Thirty years from now . . . who knows, maybe I'll be done kicking myself in the ass and will only remember the thrill of this unlikely victory. Maybe I'll only think of this guy and his house. Maybe those back-to-back home runs to Evans and Gedman will fade from my memory and I'll think only of that sustaining celebration on the mound, sipping and spilling and spraying champagne with my friends and teammates as the fans took their time leaving the stadium.

But here's what I've learned in the thirty years since that championship season: I've learned that it doesn't much matter if I'd done anything differently. We won—that's what counts, right? And besides, what could I have done differently? I'd prepared for that game, same way I always prepared. I'd tried my best, same way I always tried my best. Trouble was the other team was also prepared. They were trying, too, and they were really good. On this day, when it mattered most, they were better than me. There was a little bit more in their bats than there was in my arm, that's all. Any other game, another time on the long stretch of season, I would have fought my way through that fourth inning, given Davey Johnson a reason to leave me out there to sort through my shit, made some adjustments. I would have held on until the sixth or seventh, found some way to turn a lousy start into a mediocre start, where I would have been able to slot it in alongside the other mediocre starts I'd go on to collect and consign to that place in my thinking where they couldn't touch me.

But, no, that's not how it goes in a big spot like this. And it's not just *any* big spot—it's the biggest of the big. It's Game 7 of the World Series. Everything's on the line. Your manager can't afford to leave you out there long enough to set things right. Your teammates can't afford to wait you out. Your fans, they're only patient to a point. And so you step away from the game with the heavy footfalls of regret, and as you do you worry that it's a regret that will follow you the rest of your days. And it might . . . it just might. But would my life have gone differently if we'd lost that Game 7? Would my career have gone differently? Would I have known happiness in quite the same way?

Maybe, maybe not . . .

I couldn't know just then that this was as good as it would get for me as a professional athlete. Like I said, we were all naive enough and arrogant enough to think we'd be back on this grand stage year after year. We *expected* as much. Certainly, we had the talent to do so—and that's the shame of it. We went from what could have been one of the greatest teams in the history of the game, to a colorful group of talented athletes who managed to put together a single great season. There's a big difference, but it was a difference we could not yet know, and that's a shame, too. It's a shame for the New York Mets fans. It's a shame for the New York Mets organization. It's a shame for the city of New York and the game of baseball.

Mostly it's a shame for us, the members of that one-and-done championship team—a shame *for* us, and *on* us.

But here's the thing: because my teammates found a way to rally and get me off the hook and grab that championship trophy, every member of that 1986 New York Mets team holds a special place in the hearts and minds of our great fans—myself included. And one of the reasons I believe that team is remembered so fondly is because we found a way to win. That's all that matters, in the end. We'd put together this great season, underneath the weight of all these great expectations, and figured it all out just in time to come out on top. We put the icing on the cake—and, hey, without the icing, it's just cake, right?

INDEX

ABOUT THE AUTHORS

Ron Darling is an Emmy Award–winning baseball analyst for TBS, the MLB Network, SNY, and WPIX-TV. He was a starting pitcher for the New York Mets from 1983 to 1991 and was the first Mets pitcher to be awarded a Gold Glove. A graduate of Yale University, Darling amassed a 136–116 win-loss record during his Major League Baseball career, with 13 shutouts. He is the author of the acclaimed memoir *The Complete Game.*

Daniel Paisner has collaborated with dozens of athletes, actors, politicians, and business leaders on their autobiographies and memoirs. He is the *New York Times* bestselling coauthor of *I Feel Like Going On,* with former NFL great Ray Lewis, and *Chasing Perfect,* with Hall of Fame basketball coach Bob Hurley.